Incredible. Lutz masterfully intersects college life, theology, and discipleship in these pages. Practice what you learn here, and watch God expand his kingdom in your life and on your (his) campus.

—Brian Frye, National Collegiate Strategist,
North American Mission Board (NAMB)

Many books address kingdom, but few delve into kingdom as it pertains to studying for an exam, going to a frat party, or deciding on a major. In *King of the Campus*, Lutz offers practical and enjoyable material beneficial for any Christ-following college student.

—Abbie Smith, author of *Celibate Sex* and *Can You Keep Your Faith in College?*

If you care about helping men and women follow Jesus while they're part of the university community, you should put a copy of *King of the Campus* in their hands.

—Matt Adair, pastor of Christ Community Church in Athens, Georgia.
Director of Operations, Acts 29 Network.

King of the Campus is an important book for college students faithfully looking to make the most of their college years. Read this book with an openness and attentiveness to the active work of God in your life and on your campus. You won't regret it!

—Guy Chmieleski, University Minister at Belmont University and
author of *CAMPUS gODS* and *Shaping Their Future*.

Why did God send you to your campus? *King of the Campus* will help you discover and fulfill the answer. I highly recommend it.

—Kelly Monroe Kullberg, author of *Finding God at Harvard:
Spiritual Journeys of Thinking Christians*

KING OF THE CAMPUS

STEPHEN LUTZ

This book is dedicated to Samuel, Micah, and Abigail—
may you make Jesus Christ the King of everything!

CONTENTS

ACKNOWLEDGMENTS

No book springs from the mind of a single individual. It is the product of dozens of relationships and thousands of conversations. I wish to thank the many people who have partnered with me to shape the ministry reflected in these pages, including: Dan Nold, Stacy Sublett, Dan Dorsey, Vic King, Mike Hulson, Denny Rhule, Erica Young Reitz, Dana Ray, Josh Felstead, Kristen Arnold, Mike Swanson, Caleb Rebarchak, Andrea Redhair, Kendra Gettig, Lois Abdelmalek, Ken Hull, Ginger Larson, Sherilyn Jameson, Sara Pensyl, Scott Evans, Jonathan Weyer, Matt Stumpf, Jamie Donne, Tim and Karen Dance, Matt Adair, Brian Frye, Todd Engstrom, Tyler David, Chris Willard, Eric Mason, Kelly Monroe Kullberg, Byron Borger, Guy Chmieleski, Abbie Smith, Arliss Dickerson, Chad Logan, Paul Worcester, Connor Jennings, Tyler Changaris, Rae Bradley, Tim Hessels, Eric Augsburger, David Shultz, Drew Mohoric, Jon Tornetta, Erik Geffken, Derek Richards, Morgan Forney, Chad Oberholtzer, Aaron Henning, Alex Watlington, Andrew King, Dave Hersh, Ben Eltz, Dan Behringer, Eli Walters, Ed McCash, Mark Banker, Bob Shirey, Dave and Lisa Seibel, Chris and Colette Heinz, Dan Dupee, Sam Chez, Joel Ristuccia, Meredith Alley, Bob and Lois Andersen, Joe and Janette Cogliandro, Janet and Daniel Collier, Richard and Robyn Crane, Lee and Lyn Culver, Marc and Diane Curcillo, Eric and Sarah De Boer, Trong and Elizabeth Do, Ruth Elliott, Randall and Beth Hinton, Cathy and Ray Holsing, Debbie Holtz, Pete and Jackie Horning, Val and Hubie Hostetter, Ed and Mary Jimerson, Joe and Joyce Johnson, Don and Maureen Joos, Andrew Kalemkarian, Chrissy Kind, Justin and Kim King, Jeff and Amy Leonard, Carl and Joan Mattes, Glenn and Connie McDowell, Chad Ostrowski and Lisa Yoder, Bill and Judy Parr, Rich and Amy Ransom, Waylon and LeighShelle Robertus, Jeff and Steph Schwartz, Brad and Jenny Schwenzer, Howie and Joann Shultz, Micah and Jess Straight, Andy and Danielle Tarman, Rob and Wendy Watts, Dave and Bobbie Wenger, Dan and Mary Beth Wilkinson, the good people of Calvary Church, Elements, CommonPlace, The Five, New Life Dresher, Living Hope Church, Covenant Doylestown, and Manna Christian Fellowship. Thank you to the Willowbrook Encampment and Collective. Special thanks to Gary and Donna Schwenzer, Janet Lutz, and Ron and Sue Lutz. Great appreciation to Elizabeth Perry, Chris Folmsbee, and the House Studio team for believing in this project and helping bring it to fruition. Super special thanks to my lovely wife Jess for keeping my head on straight, my body intact, and pointing me to Jesus. You're the best!

INTRODUCTION:
"IS THIS ABOUT BEER AND SEX?"

Let me tell you about two very different friends of mine, Mindy and Matt. You might know them, or have a lot in common with them.

Mindy went to college ready to drink deeply from whatever red cup was offered to her. She had an idea of what college *should* be from talking to her friends and watching too many college movies; she also had some practice in partying as a high schooler. The thrill of being away from parental supervision and being with so many cool people was intoxicating. Mindy had some reservations at first but soon found that being a reasonably attractive freshman girl had its advantages. She had never met so many fun, interesting, and crazy people. Her freshman year was a blur, in good ways and bad. While she had a ton of fun, she had also ended up in a few compromising and regrettable situations; she did some things she'd like to forget. After a few semesters of getting grades way lower than expected, getting in a bit of legal trouble, and spending too many nights either blacked out or crying into her pillow, Mindy realized she didn't want to live this way anymore. But what other options were there? All her friends were in the party crowd.

Eventually, some people invited Mindy to a Christian group on campus. At first, the entire scene felt strange and even a little threatening to her, but the friends she made there put her at ease. Faith, and especially Jesus himself, became real and personal to her. She was at a party school, but not doing what "everyone else" was doing. Certainly, she was a lot happier than she had been in her previous lifestyle.

Mindy would never go back to her old ways, but she was unsure about what she should be doing beyond all her new Christian activities, which seemed to fill up her schedule. There were weekly meetings, Bible studies, prayer groups, service events, retreats, spring break trips, discipleship meetings with a mentor, and, oh yeah, church. The activities Mindy involved herself in were good; however, the cumulative effect had some negatives. The expectation to do so much in order to be in good standing was oppressive at times. Not only that, but the busyness seemed to crowd out her old friends, whom she saw less and less. She didn't know how to relate to them anymore, let alone share the gospel with them. And she felt constricted. Unsure what her old friends would think if she invited them into her new life, she was left wondering: Is this all she could hope for while being a Christian in college?

My friend Matt, on the other hand, had a college experience very different from Mindy. He attended a *very* conservative Bible college that prohibited hand holding with the opposite sex, and enforced things such as making your bed and a 10 P.M. curfew. Liberal only in the amount of demerits handed out for violations of their rules, the administration kept a tight rein on its students. While Matt is about the nicest, most agreeable guy you could ever meet, something about the environment, and all the rules, and the rules within the rules, encouraged his rebellious side. He wasn't a drinker, smoker, or fornicator. But breaking the rules became something of a game to him. Somehow, every semester, he accumulated nearly two hundred demerits, squeaking through with one or two less than the number that would get him automatically kicked out of the school. After dodging expulsion for not tucking in his shirt, the game got old, and he transferred to a big state university.

At first, it was one of the best things he could do for his faith. No one was checking whether his shirt was tucked in or his bed was made—it was liberating! But sure enough, he used his freedom in less than righteous ways. If pressed, he'd have to admit that *some* of the warnings he heard at Bible college had merit. He wouldn't go back to his strict life, but he felt the danger of his anything goes approach.

Matt left his strict background behind only to find that his freedom wasn't so free. Mindy left her wild days behind only to feel constricted by her Christian duty. They crossed paths but were headed in different directions. Perhaps each could have sent out a warning that the other's trajectory was dangerous, but neither had a good alternative to offer. Was bouncing between the two poles the only way to go? Was there some kind of balance in the middle, between being "free" and being "strict"?

The Two Thieves

What Matt and Mindy experienced is hardly unique to them. It's not a new problem, either. The ancient church father Tertullian once said that just as Jesus was crucified between two thieves, so the good news of Jesus is always being "crucified" between two opposing errors.

On the one side is legalism. This is what Matt reacted against and what Mindy was introduced to. We also call this moralism, or "religion." It's about getting to God by being good (however that may be defined). It's about external conformity, not inward change; changing behavior without changing the heart. It's truth without grace. It's a system that's good at creating smug, arrogant, hypocritical people, such as the Pharisees in the New Testament. It's common enough today that studies report most non-Christians see Christians this way.

On the other side of the spectrum is license. This is the "freedom" that Mindy realized was enslaving her, and what Matt was introduced to. It misunderstands grace as meaning that we can do whatever we want to do. It hates "religion," but it is religiously devoted to self, pleasure, and personal autonomy. It often assumes that we all get to God because God is so accepting of everyone (and shouldn't we be like that too?). The freedom error flouts authority, despises discipline, and is rigidly opposed to setting standards. Doling out grace without truth, it is why young people are leaving behind what Christians have believed for two thousand years in order align themselves with today's culture.

Ironically, both "thieves" end up looking the same. Inherent in both is arrogance toward God. Matt thought God should *of course* accept him, because he's been so good. Mindy thought that God should *of course* accept her, because isn't that God's job? But there's no "of course" in the gospel. The gospel combines grace *and* truth, creating humble, gracious people who love what is right. The gospel combines heart change with behavior.

The Double Bind

You might be thinking, "OK, but is this another book telling us how to stay Christian in college? Do we need more people telling us to not get drunk, not have sex, and all that stuff?"

We probably do, but this is not one of those books. While it's true that there is a whole lot more to college than beer and sex, there's also a whole lot more to college than no beer and no sex. In my years of working with college students, I've met far too many Christians who are trying to live faithfully yet feel caught in what is called a "double bind." A double bind is a situation in which you receive two conflicting messages; by affirming one you negate the other. On the one hand, the larger culture sends the message that college is a time for fun, freedom, and experimentation—a time to throw off constraints like stuffy religion. On the other hand, the message from Christian circles is a series of "don'ts." So the options, it would seem, are to dive headlong into campus culture at the expense of faithfulness, or to do what Christians tell you is obedient but boring.

Do you see how insidious the two thieves are? They are working together to keep you from joy, freedom, and purpose. The tension of this double bind is part of what causes many students to walk away from faith during their college years.

The Better Way

Amid the opportunity, life, and vitality of college, there is a better way. Different from a list of "don'ts" that leave you bored and alone on Friday night, we can have an active life that is engaged with the world around us—one that is not characterized by fear, but by faith, freedom, and joy. We *do* have a positive agenda, and it's a purpose and mission that is far greater than any campus website can promise you. What is this purpose? The kingdom of God.

While the kingdom of God includes some "don'ts," it is also much bigger than that. Big enough, in fact, to deserve your attention and energy not only for four years of college but for the rest of your life as well. We will discuss the following more in depth in chapter 2 and throughout the book, but I define the kingdom of God as: the growing presence of God's goodness and rule in our world, through Jesus Christ. On a macro scale, the kingdom is about Jesus' message being made known. Things being restored to his intentions. Wrongs being made right. Curses being reversed. Injustice being trampled, and grace and peace flourishing. On a micro scale, it's about each of us discovering our identity and calling in Christ, and becoming who God has designed us to be.

Think about the big problems on our planet right now. Wouldn't you like to see the scene change? Wouldn't you like to witness the people of God—the church—doing the things Jesus did? Wouldn't you like to see the signs of the kingdom? Sick people made well, hungry people fed, slaves and victims of oppression made free, justice and mercy instead of corruption and cruelty? These are the things Jesus claimed about himself when he read from the scroll of Isaiah in Luke 4. The kingdom of God is a huge calling. It isn't easy in the sense we usually think of easy, but one thing is for sure: *It's not boring.*

The kingdom of God explodes our double bind. As Jesus said, "The thief comes only to steal and kill and destroy; I have come that they may have life, and have it to the full" (John 10:10). Jesus warns us about the dangers of the world, but he also offers us something far better . . . abundant life through him.

Don't sell God short. There is a danger in believing that following him is a boring, dull obligation when it's actually an incredible, exhilarating, exhausting, and fulfilling journey. Even while viewing our life as a journey, many of us think that college is a rest stop—a place to get off the highway and chill for a while. However, there is meaning in every stage of our lives, including those pivotal years of school.

The kingdom of God reframes how we see college and gives us a Christian perspective. God didn't send you to school *primarily* to get an education, to make new friends, to get a good job upon graduation, or simply to pass the time until you figure out what you want to do with your life. God sent you to your campus so that you could join him in the work he's already doing there. He sent you there so you could be an agent of his kingdom, an agency he has uniquely gifted and shaped you to have. Everything you've experienced so far has been to prepare you. The kingdom of God is so much bigger and better than a handful of "don'ts." Through God's eyes, we see college

Not As:	But As:
a problem	an opportunity
somewhere to survive	somewhere to thrive/help others
something lost	something redeemed
fear-filled	faith-filled

Yes, all the beer-soaked, sex-crazed living on campus is dangerous, but it's even more dangerous for you to miss out on God's kingdom purposes. This is a book about getting in on what *really* matters. It's about not wasting your time on the counterfeits and the fakes—both secular and religious—so that you can experience and share what is true, life-giving, and fulfilling.

Here's where we are headed: Part One focuses on *Foundations of Faithfulness*. We'll deconstruct and then reform our pictures of university life from a biblical perspective, and demonstrate how the challenges we face today are nothing new but were experienced as far back as Genesis. We'll talk about the kingship of Christ and how that relates to the people and things that are worshiped on your campus. In Part Two, *The Inside-Out Kingdom*, we will look at how we are agents of the kingdom of God. The common cry of students is "to change the world," so we will discuss how that change begins with us. In this section, we will also unpack the ways transformation can happen in college, including holiness, prayer, and provocative faith. In Part Three, *Crown Him Lord of All*, we'll be introduced to a renowned theologian and university founder named Abraham Kuyper, whose concept of "sphere sovereignty" has powerful implications for how we can engage our campuses. We will study several of the spheres (or pillars) of campus life and learn about what it means for Jesus to reign as king of those areas. I've identified five pillars of campus life to focus on: church and Christian fellowship, relationships, academics and work, organizational leadership, and the party scene. Some of the spheres overlap with each other. You will likely find that you are involved in most and perhaps all of these spheres.

As we begin, I encourage you to commit this time to King Jesus. Spend some time in prayer, asking God to free you from the influence of the two thieves. In all this, my prayer is that you will leave the rest stop, get back on the journey, and faithfully engage your campus for the kingdom of God.

THE UNIVERSITY OF BABEL

Why did you come to college? Most of us arrive with dreams and aspirations more numerous than all the stuff we pack into our tiny dorm rooms. Our modern colleges and universities are incredible places to be. Yes, they may not live up to everything that the brochures, websites, and tour guides promised, but they're still exciting and full of life.

Think back to the first time you arrived on campus. What impressed you? Was it the sheer size of the campus, making you wonder how on earth you would find everything? Was it the huge, ivy-covered buildings that underscored how small and young you were by comparison? Did you notice the polished landscaping, occasionally overruled by the dirt paths carved by students determined to walk in a straight line? Did you overhear the conversations among the collectives of students, both profound and inane?

A modern campus gives off an air of bustling, ambitious sophistication, combined with sophomoric silliness and leisure. I don't know any other place quite like it. For most of us, though, the lasting impression is not the physical, architectural makeup of the campus so much as it is the *people* who populate it. It's invigorating and maybe even a bit intimidating to meet so many smart, complex people, and to discover how much drive and ambition they have. I've found that the most interesting people are not the ones who passively let college happen to them while they walk to class head-down-and-earbuds-in. The interesting ones are dreaming big and actually achieving their goals. Feeding off the energy of the campus, they are learning, innovating, and experimenting.

I remember meeting Mario my freshman year. We lived on the same floor, but my first memory of him was seeing him outside our student union building, selling bootleg T-shirts without a permit—*on our first weekend at school*. While the rest of us freshmen were still learning where the buildings were, he was setting up shop outside of them. Eventually his little business shut down, but not before making a tidy profit. I remember thinking, "This guy is going places." As I got to know Mario during that year, we talked about everything from classes to girl troubles, movie quotes, and faith. I also heard about his many business ideas. To this day, he's the most natural entrepreneur I have ever met. So I wasn't surprised a few years later when I picked up our alumni magazine and saw him featured in it, as a twenty-seven-year-old newly retired millionaire! One of his ideas had paid off, big time. Now he endows a scholarship with his name on it. In retrospect, I should have invested in his ideas back when I knew him in college.

The raw potential of everyone around you can make college a stimulating place. You may be walking around campus with future governors and senators, dot-com millionaires, CEOs, Olympic gold medalists, Nobel Prize winners, movie stars, authors, and more. Perhaps you are eating lunch with the person who will one day cure cancer. You're in class with people who will do (or maybe are already doing) unbelievable things.

Colleges, like our great cities, are incredible magnets for people with brilliance, drive, and creativity. Whenever intelligent people gather, big ideas and ambitions are sure to rise to the surface. It's always been this way, since the beginning of time.

If you grew up attending church, then you've probably heard of the Tower of Babel: humanity unites to build a tower, God gets angry and confuses their language, and they scatter, right? So the popular version goes. But let's take a look at that story in a different light, using the paradigm of the modern university. Here's the account as it appears in Genesis 11:

> Now the whole world had one language and a common speech. As people moved eastward, they found a plain in Shinar and settled there.
>
> They said to each other, "Come, let's make bricks and bake them thoroughly." They used brick instead of stone, and tar for mortar. Then they said, "Come, let us build ourselves a city, with a tower that reaches to the heavens, so that we may make a name for ourselves; otherwise we will be scattered over the face of the whole earth." But the LORD came down to see the city and the tower that the people were building. The LORD said,

"If as one people speaking the same language they have begun to do this, then nothing they plan to do will be impossible for them. Come, let us go down and confuse their language so they will not understand each other." So the LORD scattered them from there over all the earth, and they stopped building the city. That is why it was called Babel—because there the LORD confused the language of the whole world. From there the LORD scattered them over the face of the whole earth. (Vv. 1-9)

One of the first things we notice from the biblical passage is that the people who built Babel were on the move. They were nomads, attempting to create a home for themselves. Biblical commentators note that there's a good deal of insecurity running through this short story. The Babelites fear being scattered (and thus more vulnerable), so they build themselves a city. They begin working—and hard. In essence, they are hoping to find safety and security in the crowd and in what the crowd builds together. This massive building project brings in all kinds of creative types to collaborate together, from architects and engineers to businessmen and labor union leaders (or their ancient equivalents). We can assume artists are writing poems and songs about it too. Leaders emerge and give direction to the project. In their creativity, they start innovating and experimenting with new brick-making technologies and techniques. All of this work is to fuel their massive ambition, to "build ourselves a city, with a tower that reaches to the heavens."

Does this sound familiar? The college experience might easily be interchanged for the Babel story. Every fall, a new group of nomads arrives on campus. We feel incredible amounts of excitement, but also fear, insecurity, and displacement. Invariably, the freshmen contingency groups together during the first weeks of class, and we stick like glue to people we barely know. Aren't we all looking for some measure of security, out of fear of being scattered? And so we unite around a common mission—education. We begin to build. Over time, the best and the brightest rise to positions of leadership and, in the name of achievement, we invest incredible amounts of time, energy, and resources to create a better existence for ourselves and for society.

Listening to the Psycho-Babel

There is generally a dark side to unharnessed, concentrated ambition. Pride takes over. At Babel, it seemed to happen pretty quickly. The understandable desire to build something that would offer some protection quickly took on grandiose, even absurd dimensions: "Let us build ourselves a city, with a tower that reaches to the heavens, so that we may make a name for ourselves." In other words, *Let's build a tower that touches the sky and make ourselves famous! Something so impressive that people won't stop talking about us!* The people were unified, but their cause was not inherently good. And what is more important than unity alone is what the people were unified around. As one commentator noted, at Babel "depraved humanity are united in their spiritual endeavor to find, through technology, existential meaning apart from God."[1]

What's the big deal? you might be wondering. Aren't skyscrapers the modern equivalent of the Tower of Babel? It sounds like they just wanted to dream big and reach for the stars, and isn't that a basic and good human instinct? But there's more at play in the story.

In their ancient language,[2] "Babel" meant "the gate" or "residence of the gods." The people were setting themselves up as near-equals with God. The spirit of the age was, "Let's make ourselves as great as God, without needing God." Not only was this anti-God spirit expressed by their building a tower up to heaven but also by their desire to stop and cluster together. God had explicitly charged the human race with spreading out. "Be fruitful and multiply," he said, and in doing so, cause the whole earth to flourish. But the Babelites weren't spreading out. They weren't fulfilling their purpose of blessing the world. When God scatters them, his actions are not of a petulant child kicking over an anthill. He is causing people to get back in line with his good and wise plan, whether or not they feel like it.

The Babelites stopped to build because they were obsessed with achieving their own greatness. A similar spirit is alive and well in the world today, and even more concentrated on our college campuses. This culture of self-achievement feeds us lines about our greatness, and we've swallowed them whole. If you are part of the "millennial generation," roughly those born between 1981 and 2004, you have been affirmed, programmed, and coddled for greatness like no other generation in human history. Many people assume college exists simply to make you successful, rich, powerful, and famous, and that such thinking is not in conflict with the Christian faith. Yet I think this kind of "psycho-Babel" has some nasty consequences. On our campuses, we observe that the spirit of Babel results in confusion, bigger and busier self-importance, experimentation, and insecurity. So, let's look at each of these consequences in turn. If we're going to be faithful people, and if we're going to faithfully engage others in this context, we should know what we're getting into.

Confusion

What is a *university* anyway? What does it mean? In medieval Europe, groups or guilds of teachers and students gathered to promote learning, and these gatherings came to be known as *universitas*. They sought to unify people of many disciplines in the shared pursuit of knowledge. What, might we ask, are our universities unified in today? Ask students and professors in fields like biology, literature, and business some basic questions about truth, meaning, and happiness, and you will get radically different answers. There isn't much *uni* in *university* anymore. Meaning, there is no *one* consensus or goal. That project has in many ways collapsed.

It's largely unknown, but many of the original universities in North America were founded as places to train pastors for ministry. The idea was a strong one, that pastors (and others) should have an understanding of ancient languages, philosophy, math and science, literature, and other disciplines alongside their theology. Over time, university leadership did away with the pastoral training component and, eventually, decided to pursue knowledge without God as the source and goal of their knowledge. In the words of Paul, "They exchanged the truth about God for a lie, and worshiped and served created things rather than the Creator—who is forever praised" (Romans 1:25).

Let me give you just one example. Harvard was founded in 1636 as a school to train Christian ministers. In 1692 it adopted the motto "Veritas Christo et Ecclesiae," which in Latin means "Truth for Christ and the Church." Take a closer look at the original seal, and you'll notice the top two books on the shield are facing up, but the book on the bottom is facing down. In this way, the seal was to be a symbolic reminder of the limits of human reason and the need for God's revealed truth. At some point, however, Harvard changed its motto, shortening it simply to *Veritas*, without all the religious stuff. All three books in the modern Harvard seal now face upward, as if there is no limit to human reason. This is but one example of how universities decided to remove God as the *telos* (or goal, purpose) of their learning. A similar secularizing process played out, again and again, across the country. People built their towers of "truth," assuming it was possible to know nearly as much as God, without needing God. Is it any coincidence that we sometimes refer to academia as the "ivory tower"?

There have been some interesting and tragic effects of removing God from the academic mission. For starters, when there is no unifying goal or *telos* at a university, any number of "created things" compete to be worshiped and pursued, whether it is knowledge, power, riches, or pleasure. The options for alternative gods are as many and varied as creation itself. There's no one way, no *uni* anymore. We are not on one search; we are on many searches, disagreeing on how best to go about it. It's no wonder people feel lost and confused. At the very least, it accounts for why students are undecided and change their majors so often.

While the original residents of Babel named their city as "the gateway of the gods," the Hebrews who wrote the Bible got the last laugh, because Babel sounds like the Hebrew word for confusion (not to mention our English "babble"). Just like the builders of Babel eventually departed in confusion, so will many of today's students. Despite undoubtedly successful attempts to increase our knowledge in general, the university lacks a framework or overarching purpose for that knowledge. The result is thousands of voices attempting to shout over one another and, ultimately, too many confused generations of students.

Bigger and Busier Self-Importance

Nobody likes the guy who takes himself a little too seriously. You whisper under your breath, "Hey, *relax*! You're not that big of a deal!" But have you ever said that about a building? The University of Pittsburgh's campus is dominated by a building called the Cathedral of Learning. Standing at 535 feet tall, it's the tallest educational building in the Western Hemisphere. As the term *cathedral* implies, it operates like a church. However, instead of being dedicated to the worship of God, it is dedicated to the worship of knowledge. It's rumored that the Cathedral of Learning intentionally lacks a steeple, since the steeple on a church is traditionally intended to point up to the heavens and acknowledge God. Your campus probably doesn't contain a skyscraper, but I bet it has at least one building designed to take your breath away; perhaps a building meant to impress visitors on those campus tours. I have no problem with stately structures, but it's worth asking, "Where does my school take itself a little too seriously?"

Excellence is important, and the artisanship and labor that goes into making beautiful buildings is a good thing. However, the condition of our hearts as we work, study, and play inside of these buildings determines whether or not they become our churches, our places of worship. Are we unknowingly becoming the priests of self-importance? Self-importance can take a lot of forms, one of the most common being busyness. We run from class to meeting to working out to a quick meal and then on to more before crashing into our beds, only to get far too little sleep. Why? Because busyness is one of the ways we prove to ourselves and others how important we are. I've observed far too many students who are incredibly high achieving and skilled, but they lack integrity, substance, and a core. They're busy, but they feel hollow.

Years ago, the evangelist Billy Graham visited Harvard University and was talking with then-president Derek Bok. Graham asked, "What's the biggest problem facing college students?" Bok answered succinctly, "Emptiness." I don't think much has changed. We may be busy, but we lack substance. We've programmed ourselves to be efficient automatons of achievement, but to what end? Much of our achievement has lacked meaning. I've seen too many students running exhaustedly on the treadmill of success, only to crash and realize that their busyness was an attempt to avoid deeper, harder issues.

Bigger and busier is not always better. Our society—and university culture with it—is like those giant, genetically modified strawberries that we pick up from the grocery store. They're huge, they're red, but they're hollow and nearly tasteless. If you have a *real* strawberry, a natural one from your garden or a farmer's market, you immediately taste the difference. The modified strawberries have the general form and function of a fruit, but we find that they are distorted, less tasty, and ultimately less appealing than how God intended. That's human nature. That's Babel. That could be college, unless . . .

Experimentation

I mentioned earlier that I love the college atmosphere: the energy, the excitement, the willingness to try new things, and the fresh ideas. But it has its ugly sides. Colleges are like our greatest cities. They are uniquely able to put the best and worst of society on display, often simultaneously and side by side. In a big city, disparity might look like homeless people sitting out in front of a world-class theater or art gallery. Or a renowned university with billion dollar endowments next to underfunded public high schools whose graduates barely have fifth grade reading levels. On campus, we find students who give time and energy to participating in peace rallies or fighting for social justice by day, yet see nothing wrong with sexually exploiting a fellow human being by night.

We're told that the value of the college experience is in trying new things. Experiment. Branch out. Seek new experiences, some will say. College is like one big laboratory, so have fun! Yet not every experiment is worth trying. As Mary Shelley's *Frankenstein* (and other famous plotlines) have emphasized, certain experiments can have unforeseen, and undesirable, consequences. The people of Babel were experimenters and innovators, building their tower in the form of bricks and tar instead of stone. Innovation can be worthwhile, but as any savvy Hebrew reader would recognize, bricks later came to symbolize the oppression and slavery that the Hebrews faced in Egypt under Pharaoh. As so often happens, our experiments turn on us. They are not as benign as we think. We believe we have control of them, only to find that they control us; and we often find out too late. Yes, the atmosphere of college is like a laboratory, but sometimes *we* are the ones being experimented on. "Let's see if this works" is a lot less appealing when you're the subject. The frequency of alcohol-related sexual assault on campuses is proof that all experimentation is not harmless. What happens in the name of experimentation can be exploitative.

God responds to Babel's great experiment in self-importance. On one level, what they're doing is pathetic. Build a tower that reaches to heaven? Yeah right. God has to come down, verse 5 says, just to see it. That's how small it is compared to the heavenlies. On the other hand, God is also aware of humanity's tremendous capacity to inflict harm on ourselves. "The LORD said, 'If as one people speaking the same language they have begun to do this, then nothing they plan to do will be impossible for them. Come, let us go down and confuse their language so they will not understand each other'" (Genesis 11:6-7).

Consider the last hundred years of world history: two world wars (and countless others), genocides, terrorism, government-sponsored famine, economic oppression, and more slavery in the world today than at any point in human history. There are nearly seven thousand languages spoken in the world today, but imagine what we would do to each other if we didn't have the language barriers? "Nothing they plan to do will be impossible for them." Aren't you glad Hitler, Stalin, and Mao had some resistance to their experiments?

Perhaps you are seeing now why God steps in at Babel and confuses their language. He wasn't being petty, vindictive, or insecure when he scattered humankind; he intervened because he loved us. It was a mercy. He was saving us from ourselves. There are plenty of people walking around our campuses, perhaps you included, who are reaping the consequences of experiments gone wrong. But God's mercy is greater than our mistakes, and he's not done with us yet.

Collective Insecurity

Vampires, werewolves, and zombies. Not only is this the stuff of our nightmares, but it's the stuff of our entertainment as well. Mythological monsters have made a comeback in recent years, a trend that has been lucrative for authors, producers, and actors. According to culture watchers, these gruesome characters have become symbols of our collective insecurity. They serve as allegorical avatars for our fears.

Our best building projects, all the things that we've placed our hopes in to make us great and to save us, are showing their weak points. It feels like the towers of money, government, education, and climate are coming down, to name just a few. The only constant now is change, and that fact leaves us feeling a bit insecure. Because of our access to around-the-clock global news sources, we hear about human disaster and hardship like never before. It seems like the sky is always falling for someone. We just hope it never happens to us.

September 11, 2001, was a reminder that all towers come down, eventually. Except one. "The name of the LORD is a strong tower; the righteous run into it and are safe" (Proverbs 18:10, NRSV).

Babelites thought themselves the center of the world, and we have a tendency to do the same. In our own minds, we often think we are doing something great, but Jesus' definition of greatness is very different:

Jesus called them together and said, "You know that those who are regarded as rulers of the Gentiles lord it over them, and their high officials exercise authority over them. Not so with you. Instead, whoever wants to become great among you must be your servant, and whoever wants to be first must be slave of all. (Mark 10:42-44)

The human assumption, expressed at Babel, is that greatness is achieved through growing bigger and building higher. Jesus turns this thinking upside down. He ultimately showed us what greatness is by making himself low. We can't build our way up to heaven, but in Christ, heaven has come down to us. When Jesus came as a baby, he arrived in humility. But when he comes again, he will come in glory. Revelation 21 tells us that the entire Holy City of God will descend one day, in all its beauty and glory. God comes down to us!

Just like at Babel, the dominant worldview on your campus is that greatness is found through puffing ourselves up, ambition should have no limits, and our security lies in how much stuff we own. Jesus reverses our assumptions by showing us instead that greatness is found in humility, that we should seek first the kingdom of God and his righteousness, and that if we want to save our lives, we need to lose them. The way up is down. It's the great reversal.

Only the power of the gospel can truly reverse what happened at Babel. In the babble created by competing worldviews, Christians need to speak and live as the very presence of Christ on our campuses, bringing words of hope to a confused people. Where people once found unity around selfish ambition, we can demonstrate unity around Jesus Christ. Through Christ, we can live lives of humility, generosity, and sacrifice. The reversal and redemption of Babel is foreshadowed in Zephaniah 3:9, where it says, "Then will I purify the lips of the peoples, that all of them may call on the name of the LORD and serve him shoulder to shoulder."

These prophetic words begin to manifest themselves in Acts 2. Through the supernatural work of the Holy Spirit, the gospel is proclaimed in the various languages of the world. Many languages are spoken, but all with the same message. Words of hope and good news begin to reach the scattered peoples of the world. True to God's original intent, the people are scattered throughout the world, so that every tongue can call on the Lord, serve him shoulder to shoulder, and build something of eternal value: the kingdom of God.

What Tower Are You Building?

Why did you come to college? To eventually qualify for a good job? To make lots of money? To have fun? To earn recognition? Or perhaps it just seemed like the next thing to do? These are some of the common stories we are (often unconsciously) living in. What towers are we building? If we're not intentionally asking ourselves hard questions, it's likely that we're building our own towers—towers of success, achievement, money, power, reputation, pleasure, and more. But God has something much better in mind for us than our sand castles. The biblical story should reshape how we view our college years. You are not *gathering* on your specific campus, at this specific time, so that you can become great. You are, however, being *sent* there by God for a good and unique purpose. You may be enrolled at the University of Babel, but you belong to a different kingdom.

You might be reading this, thinking, "I don't buy into the ambition and pride of my campus. I spend a lot of my time with my ministry, church, or fellowship group, doing God-honoring things." But here's my concern. It's possible to imbibe the spirit of Babel and express it in Christian-looking ways. Our religious ambitions and arrogance are expressed through building the "towers" of our own little groups. Seeking safety and security, we never leave our small circles of friends. It's easy to look out for our own comfort, instead of willingly being scattered to the corners of the campus, for the flourishing of all. If we don't approach our campus with a sense of being *sent* to it, in Jesus' name, then we're just baptizing Babel.

Being sent to the scattered means being concerned with advancing God's kingdom, not building our own. It means struggling against the pride and ambition that is all around us. Being sent also means we may look very different from those around us even as we look for true security in God. For instance, we will need to rightly direct our ambition, and use the knowledge, technology, and tools that we gain at school for God's purposes, not ours. We should create and innovate with the mission of increasing the knowledge of God, and seeing our campus flourish. We should also seek to be a blessing, bringing the peace of God into hard and dark places.

To follow Christ means a certain amount of downward mobility. Maybe we won't have people trumpeting our successes from the rooftops (or the tower). Maybe we won't be famous or rich or voted most likely to succeed. Even if our names won't be great, *God's name will*. And that's better by far.

CHAPTER 1

Discussion Questions

1. Why did you come to college? Have your reasons changed?

2. What are the "Towers of Babel" on your campus? What traits make something Babel-ish?

3. In the chapter we listed four areas that result in "psycho-Babel": *Confusion*, a *Bigger and Busier* mentality, *Experimentation*, and *Insecurity*. Which of these do you relate to most? Why?

4. Your friends, classmates, classes, and clubs are building Babel; how can you show them something better, and invite them into building the kingdom of God?

WHO'S KING OF THE CAMPUS?

TWO

Back in the day, BMOC referred to the "Big Man on Campus." He's the guy everyone pays attention to. People listen to what he says and like the stuff he likes. He's lavished with attention and praise. He sets the tone, and the rest of us follow. Even if the term has changed, campuses today still have a few BMOCs and BWOCs (Woman): the quarterback of the football team, the sorority president, the president of student government, or the editor of the paper or blog that everyone reads. One thing about these BMOCs/BWOCs—they know they're influential. They enjoy the attention they receive. After all, they're the kings (and queens) of the campus.

Maybe campuses today don't have as clearly identifiable "royalty" as they have in the past. But make no mistake; whether or not we can easily spot them, campuses still have kings. The BMOCs/BWOCs come and go, but the objects or ideas they represent have tremendous staying power. The functional kings of the campus are probably not people, but rather whatever people are living for, or whatever they willingly give their time, energy, and money to.

Here's one example of a king on many campuses, and it's a powerful one: the party scene. This king gets people to dress up in revealing clothes so they can hang out with people they don't really know or like and do things they never thought they would do. Some of them end their night with the infamous "walk of shame" or "worshiping at the porcelain throne." Worship, indeed. Kings get people to do some crazy things.

True Worship

It's not overstating things to say that all our behaviors are acts of worship. That is, our actions reveal what we love, value, and serve. The biblical idea of worship is much bigger and broader than we usually think. In the Old Testament, the Hebrew word *Avodah* is commonly used and often translated as "worship" in our Bibles. It does not strictly refer to what we commonly think of as worship though, e.g., singing in a large group. Avodah has a strong sense of *service*. In other words, we worship what we serve, and we serve what we worship.

Worship is not exclusive to "religious people." We are all worshipers. Every one of us worships something or someone. As humans, we are relentless in our desire to worship, and campuses are full of temples, shrines, and idols dedicated to the worship of all kinds of things.

Human nature being what it is, campus kings will invariably include:

- Knowledge and academic success
- Status and fame
- Power and influence
- Pleasure and sex
- Money and things

The things that become idolatrous often start out as good things. In fact, good things become the most troublesome of idols. Tim Keller says idolatry is taking a good thing and making it an ultimate thing. It's putting a good thing in the place only Jesus should occupy.

When we abuse and pervert these gifts, we get in trouble. God gave us brains so that we could grow in knowledge—but then we try to seek knowledge apart from him as if we don't need him. God gave us the ability to lead, and to rule his creation as stewards, but then we forget him and hurt people and abuse his world. God gave us sex for enjoyment and as a powerful expression of oneness, but then we ignore his design and harm others as well as ourselves.

In all these things, we are setting up something else in the place of God. We are worshiping something else as king. We have broken the first commandment, "You shall have no other gods before me" (Exodus 20:3). Our shrines and statues on campus easily become a violation of the second commandment: "You shall not make for yourself an image in the form of anything in heaven above or on the earth beneath or in the waters below. You shall not bow down to them or worship them; for I, the LORD your God, am a jealous God" (Exodus 20:4-5).

What does this mean? On our campuses (and in our own hearts), people are committing treason against the King of the Universe. It's rampant, happening all around us, all the time. Instead of ultimate allegiance to the King, we've set up some side deals with other "gods." For Jesus to be King on our campuses, these idols need to be dethroned. They need to be taken down—maybe even literally.

Taking Down Statues

I serve with students at Penn State University, which is also my alma mater. You might remember that Penn State was in the news a lot during the end of 2011 and throughout 2012. When it became known that Jerry Sandusky, a popular and respected former assistant football coach, had committed unspeakable crimes against children, it felt as if our world exploded.

Suddenly, every news outlet you could imagine descended on our little college town, with their satellite trucks and reporters. Every hour brought a new revelation or rumor. Shock gave way to shame, anger, and fear. Only a few days earlier, "JoePa," the beloved and legendary football coach Joe Paterno, had gained his all-time best 409th win. But late on a Wednesday night, he was fired, along with the university president. The two men who had without a doubt the most influence in town were now kicked to the curb. Watching the coverage in disbelief that night on CNN, I saw several thousand students spontaneously gather in front of the administration building in protest, then start running en masse downtown to act out their anger. They did millions of dollars of damage, flipping over a TV van and damaging storefronts.

What happened at Penn State was tragic and complicated. I don't believe the full story has been told (nor do I have the space to do that here), but I do believe idolatry is one aspect of the story. What was our idol in this case? Our collective sense of identity, which was wrapped up in all that Penn State football and the university had come to mean for so many of us. We were enthralled with our reputation for combined academic accomplishment and on-field success. *Success with honor* is the phrase we used, and it's what we meant when our more than 100,000 fans cheered, "We are . . . Penn State!" We had the sense of not being like "all those other schools." It was what we boasted in. And then, almost overnight, it was gone.

Have you ever been in a situation where an entire community goes through the stages of grief together? For me, this was one of the most stressful and surreal weeks I've ever experienced. The aftermath lasted for months and will likely continue for years. Two months after he was fired, JoePa was dead from lung cancer. Then they took down his statue, one of the shrines on our campus.

You Gotta Serve Somebody

Those of us at Penn State got an intensive course in the consequences of sin, but we learned what everyone learns sooner or later. Human nature is to serve someone or something. It's as natural to us as the mysterious longing for Someone outside ourselves. God gave us knees to bow down. We are made to serve. This was depicted well in the movie *The Avengers*. Loki descends on Stuttgart, Germany, and starts zapping and killing people, before speaking:

> Loki [to crowd]: Kneel before me. I said . . . KNEEL! Is not this simpler? Is this not your natural state? It's the unspoken truth of humanity that you crave subjugation. The bright lure of freedom diminishes your life's joy in a mad scramble for power. For identity. You were made to be ruled. In the end, you will always kneel.
> German Old Man [stands]: Not to men like you.
> Loki: There are no men like me.
> German Old Man: There are always men like you.

What made that scene eerily compelling was that it has the ring of truth. Notice the German man doesn't disagree with Loki's assertion that we will always kneel. What he bravely resists is kneeling down to an obviously evil entity like Loki. (Presumably, as an older German, he knows what happens when we kneel to someone like that.)

The whole scene is reminiscent of Daniel's refusal to pray to King Darius in Daniel 6. He opened the windows and reserved his prayers for God alone. For that, he is thrown in the lions' den, but ultimately saved. Loki was half-right. We *will* always kneel. As the philosopher Goethe once said, "None are more hopelessly enslaved than those who falsely believe they are free." Or, as another wise sage (Bob Dylan) once sang, "You're gonna have to serve somebody."

Deep down, we all know we will serve someone or something. We like to foster the illusion that we control our own destinies, but eventually we discover otherwise. We look to things like success, sex, power, and status, like they are jewels in our crowns. They are powerful, but we think we can keep them under control, only to eventually find that they are controlling us. We will always kneel. The question isn't *if* you have a king (or kings), but which one(s). Are you serving the *right* king, the King of Kings?

The search for a king is a theme running through Scripture. The Bible tells an interesting story about Israel and its desire for a king, an authority. You might think God would be on board with this. "Finally, maybe we can get some law and order around here!" But when they ask for a king, via Samuel (the last judge), God instructs Samuel to tell them what having a king will mean for them and their descendants: oppression, corruption, and worse.

Wait, didn't they need a king? Why such a negative forecast? Here's the problem, they had rejected their true King, God himself. Only God is qualified for the job. Among all the nations of the earth, they had the unique opportunity to be ruled by the King of Kings, and they rejected him. They chose to be like all the other nations instead and had to deal with the consequences. Barring a few notable exceptions (like David), most of the kings who followed were more like Loki.

I Thought We Were Into Democracy

You might be thinking, "What's with all this talk about kings? Aren't we supposed to be into democracy? Aren't there limits on how far we can take this king metaphor?"

C. S. Lewis was British, so we would expect him to have more of an affinity for the Crown, but he believed in democracy, and not for the reasons you might think:

A great deal of democratic enthusiasm descends from the ideas of people like Rousseau, who believed in democracy because they thought mankind so wise and good that everyone deserved a share in the government. The danger of defending democracy on those grounds is that they're not true. . . . I find that they're not true without looking further than myself. I don't deserve a share in governing a hen-roost, much less a nation. . . . The real reason for democracy is . . . Mankind is so fallen that no man can be trusted with unchecked power over his fellows. Aristotle said that some people were only fit to be slaves. I do not contradict him. But I reject slavery because I see no men fit to be masters.[1]

Lewis is saying that democracy is an admission of our weaknesses as human beings, not our strengths. It's a way to limit the damage one person can do.

But if we could find a king who was not fatally flawed by sin, and who would rule over his subjects with great power *and* great love, then a king would be the way to go, right? If we could look to a leader like that—with no weakness, no folly, no sin—then we would never want to vote that person out of office.

Spoiler alert: Jesus is the true King we're looking for.

Who Is Jesus?

Jesus is qualified to be our King. He's the real deal. He is not just from the royal line of David, but he's the King of Kings. "In him all things were created . . . all things have been created through him and for him" (Colossians 1:16). He's first in the resurrection. He's the head of his body, the church. He's also her bridegroom. He holds all things together. He's central to the story of redemption. He's undoubtedly the most influential person in history. He's present on the first page and the last page of the Bible. Read John 1, Colossians 1, and Hebrews 1, and you get a sense of just how awe-inspiring and all-encompassing he is. Jesus Christ is the hope of nations, the champion who has defeated all challengers, the King of Kings.

But do we think of him that way?

I fear that we've dishonored him by shrinking him down. Yes, Jesus is our friend and brother. Both of those are biblical. But that's not all he is. Jesus is also King. He is Savior. He is God. It is staggering that Jesus is our friend and brother, and that he is among us and wants to know us. It's incredible *precisely because* he's also the King. Amid all the idolatry on our campuses, it's not enough to say that Jesus is our friend and homeboy. He must be declared King.

The declaration of Jesus as Savior and King is commonly referred to as "the gospel," which means simply "good news." The word for this in the New Testament Greek is *euangelion,* from which we get our word "evangelical." But this word did not originate with Christians. Greek rulers since Alexander the Great issued "gospels." Roughly thirty years before Jesus' birth, the Roman world was filled with conflict and sectarian violence. When Caesar Augustus came to power and defeated the forces of Marc Antony and Cleopatra, messages went out all over the empire, declaring him to be a god. One declaration said, "Providence . . . by producing Augustus [has sent] us and our descendants a Savior, who has put an end to war and established all things."[2] Sound familiar?

The expectation was that hearers of these proclamations would believe and worship the one who was the source of the good news, identify themselves with him and his kingdom, and show all allegiance to him. So, when Jesus comes along, and he and his followers begin to proclaim a different gospel, this is no small claim. It was radical, and it was subversive. Contrary to the emperor's claims, the gospel of Jesus proclaimed that:

1. True **belief** is that Jesus (not any other human being or created thing) is God, Savior, and King.

2. True **worship** is due to King Jesus, and him alone.
3. True **identity** is found in Jesus and his kingdom, which is eternal and transcendent.
4. True **allegiance** belongs to King Jesus and his kingdom, against all other rivals.

This gospel was radical then and it is radical now. Whether it's the rivals of Rome or the rival gods on campus, Jesus' rightful place is to be enthroned above all others in the hearts of his people—against all other contenders, pretenders, and counterfeits. We belong to him—he deserves our love, worship, and allegiance. And this relationship is what a true announcement of the gospel of Jesus proclaims.

Stewards, Not Sovereigns

What does it mean for us to be kingdom people? It means our allegiance has shifted. It means we will live in a different way from those around us, because we worship a different king. It means we recognize not only our King, but also his kingdom, and our role in it.

There's a great scene in the film adaptation of J. R. R. Tolkien's novel, *The Return of the King*, when Gandalf and Pippin enter the throne room of Gondor. There they encounter Denethor, steward of Gondor. The stewards were a line of rulers entrusted with protecting Gondor until the rightful king should return. Two thrones dominate the room: one high up on a pedestal for the king, the other on the floor for the steward. Denethor sits on the lower throne, but it's obvious that long ago he mentally transitioned to the upper throne. He has stopped acting as a steward, and started acting like a sovereign. When confronted by Gandalf, he declares, "I will not bow to this Ranger from the North, last of a ragged house long bereft of lordship." Gandalf replies, "Authority is not given to you to deny the return of the king, steward!" Denethor shows just how far he's fallen when he angrily responds, "The rule of Gondor is mine and no other's!"

As humans, we have been given the role of steward, not king. It's Jesus' kingdom, not ours! It is all too easy to take authority that does not belong to us. We easily forget who we are and *whose* we are. Do that long enough, and we won't long for the King to return—we won't even recognize him when he appears.

For Jesus Christ to be King on our campuses, these idols must first be identified and dethroned in the hearts of his followers. "In your hearts revere Christ as Lord" (1 Peter 3:15). When brought before the King, stewards submit. They literally kneel. What's your posture toward Jesus?

CHAPTER 2

SCRIPTURE STUDY: Psalm 96

Discussion Questions

1. What are the places of worship on your campus, and what is worshiped there?

2. The author says, "Human nature is to serve someone or something. God gave us knees to bow down." Do you agree? Where do you see evidence of this in your own life or in the lives of others?

3. How do you most often view Jesus? Do you think of him as a best friend or King of the Universe? Why are both important?

4. In what ways are you living as a steward or sovereign?

Further Reading: *Counterfeit gods*, Tim Keller

THREE RETURN TO THE KING

Kings have kingdoms. Jesus' kingdom extends to and includes the college campus. Kings also have subjects. At least, the real kings do. You may declare yourself the "King of Madden" or the "Queen of Pinterest," but that title probably doesn't lead to thousands of people cheering your name.

Jesus is the King of everything, even if not everyone acknowledges it (yet). But we know where history is heading:

God has highly exalted him and bestowed on him the name that is above every name, so that at the name of Jesus every knee should bow, in heaven and on earth and under the earth, and every tongue confess that Jesus Christ is Lord, to the glory of God the Father. (Philippians 2:9-11, ESV)

One day *every* knee will bow. But some of us aren't waiting until that last day to bow the knee. We are choosing now to live sneak previews of coming attractions. In a world that is serving many other kings, we live as servants of the King of Kings. So if Jesus is our King, and the rightful recipient of our love, honor, and service, what does that look like?

I Surrender All

I've met some interesting students over the years, with some interesting ideas about how life works. One of my student leaders approached me one day with a concerned expression. She began, "My friend is really into knowing what God's will is, and surrendering to that." So far, so good, I'm thinking. She continued, "He literally wants to know God's will for *every* decision he makes. For example, he'll stand at the sink in the morning and ask God if he wants him to brush his teeth that day." The creases on her face deepened as she asked me, "What do you think of that?"

I smiled and replied, "I think it's great that he wants to live his life so intimately surrendered to Jesus. But" (you knew there was a "But" coming), I said, "I think God wants him to brush his teeth. I think we know God's will on this. For one thing, brushing our teeth, as well as other practices of personal hygiene, are one way we fulfill the commandment to love our neighbor. And I'm pretty sure not only God wants him to brush his teeth, but so do his girlfriend, his roommates, his professors, and society in general. God gave him a brain—he should use it. God gave him teeth—he should keep them."

Sometimes surrendering to God's will isn't as hard or mysterious as we make it out to be. (I never got confirmation on whether God sometimes told him to not brush his teeth.) As extreme as that one student's experience is, I wonder if we are all extremists in our own ways. Does God look at us and ask, "My children, why do you make it so complicated? Stop standing in front of the mirror, and start doing what I've designed for you to do." He's already told us what a surrendered life looks like. Jesus says, "If anyone would come after me, let him deny himself and take up his cross and follow me" (Mark 8:34, ESV).

The life of following Jesus means taking up our cross. It means identifying with Jesus, even to the point of suffering. It means killing any desires or ambitions that are opposed to him. It means denying ourselves. Do you see what this means? You can't follow God and stay where you are. The cross means movement.

We're not just talking about big things. For a lot of us, the challenge is most deeply felt in the thousands of little decisions we make every day, where we consciously decide to adjust our will to align with God's. We're making many course corrections along the way, lots of minor adjustments that together add up to something radical. The word "adjustment" is a bit risky, of course. I don't want you to misunderstand me. When I say adjustment, you might think we're talking about simply tweaking something. I went to the chiropractor recently and got an adjustment—C6 always falls out, and he pops it back in, boom, I'm good. It's a minor adjustment, takes twenty minutes. But that's not the kind of adjustment Jesus is talking about. No, he's calling us to major changes, to bring *everything* into alignment with Christ. He becomes the center. The true north. Everything is reoriented around him.

The Relief of Surrender

While part of us bristles at Jesus' claim to our very lives, we need to remember that the King is entitled to do this. He's the Creator. He's the Redeemer. And he's the one in charge. But this isn't a power trip for him. He also does this for our good. He calls us to surrender because he knows it's the best thing for us.

So he puts this decision in front of us, essentially saying, "You can spend your time, energy, money, and ambition on trying to find life now, and you will lose it; or you can lose your life for me and the gospel, giving your life to me for safekeeping, and you will find it. You can't have it all—you must choose."

Which is the better decision, eternally speaking? The challenge Jesus lays out is a particularly difficult one for us. We're conditioned to think that we can "have it our way," "be anything we want to be," and generally have it all. Jesus cuts through those lies. He's asking us to think with some perspective and to consider the short-term against the long-term. In case we don't get what he's offering, he puts it another way: "What good is it for someone to gain the whole world, yet forfeit their soul?" (Mark 8:36). He's saying, "What I have to offer your soul is better than anything this world—even the entire world itself—has to offer!" That's what business folks call cost-benefit analysis, and it's a decision Jesus places right in front of us. If we truly understand the costs versus the benefits, it shouldn't even be a tough choice. But it is.

I recently watched a documentary that detailed how a majority of pro athletes are broke only three years after they stop playing. It's like the lottery syndrome. They're flush with cash, but a combination of excess, bad decisions, scams, and leeches leaves most of them penniless. It's easy to watch that and say, "How foolish. If I made $5 million a year, I'd do better than that. They should know better than to blow it on five houses, fifteen cars, and all that stuff."

Then I realized, spiritually speaking, we are all like that. Isn't that what Jesus is saying? We are flush with this currency called *life*, but because we don't know how to wisely consider the long-term, we risk blowing it.

Typically, when faced with Jesus' challenge to take up our cross we only register how hard it is. However, the underlying call is that we give control over to the one who knows best. I spoke with a guy recently who was considering Christianity, and he asked, "So you're saying I wouldn't be in charge of my life?" After I confirmed his statement, he continued, "I've always felt as if it were up to me to make the right decisions. But you're saying I can trust God with my life?" Nod. "Well, if that's true, that would be a huge relief!" When I heard him say that, I knew he was getting close. A few weeks later, he surrendered his life to Jesus, with great joy.

When we surrender our lives to Jesus, we learn the relief of surrender. We're finally entrusting our lives to the one who is qualified to handle them. We experience peace, because we can trust the one to whom we've surrendered. We become confident, because we have the King of the Universe looking out for us. Surrender gives us life without regrets, because we know his plan is best.

When I face the end of my life, I want to do so with peace, confidence, and no regrets. I want to stand before God, and say, "I surrendered. I lost a lot. I gave up a lot. I sacrificed a lot. I even suffered a lot. But it was worth it." So many of us are on the brink of that. Some of us stand on the bubble of faith. We like Jesus, and we draw some encouragement from his love and forgiveness. But we haven't surrendered. We stand on the edge of living for something worth dying for, and perhaps even dying for something worth living for. At one level, we know that there's no contest when it comes to choosing between "the world" and our soul. Yet we're afraid to take that next crucial step of surrendering to Jesus.

Vampire Christianity

Why do we linger at the starting line when Jesus calls us into the race? One reason is that we may believe in a false version of Christianity, something less than the call that Jesus gives. Instead of this dynamic invitation to leave everything to follow Christ, we've become what Dallas Willard calls Vampire Christians—people "who only want a little blood for their sins but nothing more to do with Jesus until heaven."[1] Basically, "I'll take your life, Jesus, but I won't give you mine."

How can we possibly reject the call of King Jesus? We compartmentalize him. We keep him at arm's length. We limit the demands he can make. Not surprisingly, our experience of Jesus becomes limited. He seems a lot less relevant to us and our situation. Then we wonder why this Jesus thing isn't compelling.

But King Jesus doesn't cooperate with our attempts to put him in a box. I have a friend who is the president of his fraternity. He grew up in a Christian setting, but when he got to college, he chose the party life—booze, parties, girls, and more. He didn't completely repudiate his faith, but he acted like it. During his third semester, he realized how empty all the partying was. He didn't like what it was doing to him, or the person he was becoming. He's been finding his way back to faith over the past year.

When I asked him how Christianity had been portrayed to him as he grew up, he described this vampire Christianity, nothing very compelling or urgent in the here and now. And that's why he walked away. But all along he'd been look-ing for a life worth dying for, not some Chicken Soup for the Soul. He'd watch movies like *Gladiator*, *300*, and numerous WWII movies, wondering, "Where can *I* find that?"

It's not enough when as Christians we're merely skimming the surface of life, striking up a measly bargain between warm fuzzies and occasional moral checkpoints. No wonder we get bored and walk away from faith. But remember, this is not the covenant that Jesus offers. You've probably heard the statistics about young people leaving the faith. Headlines read: "Christianity is declining." But this is only partly true. *Casual Christianity* is declining. Yes, some people are opting out; people who used to check the box next to Christian because they're not Jewish or Muslim are now checking None. The ones who are "leaving Christianity" are leav-ing a truncated, watered down, vampire Christianity. And who can blame them? It's simply not compelling.

Here's the thing: When people read their Bibles more, pray more, go to church more, are involved in other meetings like Bible studies and small groups—these Christians live lives that are markedly different from others. In other words, the more their relationship with God shows up in their daily life, the more committed and vital their faith commitment is. What we need are more Christians who have taken up their cross and demonstrate that we have something worth living and dying for!

Everyday Radicals

What does daily-life Christianity look like? Often, we expect to be called to something radical, something incredible and over the top. When my mom was young, her church had a traveling missionary come and speak, telling tales about the tribe he reached in the African jungle. Someone has to reach that tribe. But it's unlikely that *all* of us will. We will all be called to step out of our comfort zones, to die to self, to do hard things out of allegiance to our King. But we not only need acts of extreme or radical devotion but also need everyday faithfuls—people living lives of simple, everyday fidelity.

When I was in college, I faced one of those relatively insignificant decisions that shaped me profoundly. I became the main worship leader for our Christian group on Wednesdays and Sundays. This meant a lot of singing, which was fine . . . except for Sunday mornings in the fall. On Saturdays, we often had football games to go to, which meant a lot of cheering, yelling, screaming, and singing. I was passionately devoted to being a fan. But I quickly discovered that I didn't have those iron lungs that would let me scream my guts out on Saturday and still have a voice left on Sunday. So I was faced with a fundamental decision, and it was as if God put the decision to me this way: "Steve, who will you use your voice for? To cheer on Saturday or to worship on Sunday?" Eventually, I chose worship. I had to work hard to not yell and shout and cheer like I used to. It was hard! Surprisingly, the other one hundred thousand plus fans didn't seem to notice, and neither did the football team. But God did. And so did I. Years later, I can say it was a pivotal moment for my walk with him.

What Are You Afraid Of?

When we get down to the reason why most of us keep Jesus at arm's length, we find fear. We fear following him will be too difficult and too costly, that we'll have to give up too much. We fear what other people think, not wanting to become (or be called) a "Jesus Freak." We fear being disappointed and wonder whether the required effort is worthwhile.

We would do well to remind ourselves of stories of people who have given up more than we have and could still say, "It is worth it." I came across the story of a woman named Rosaria Champagne Butterfield. She tells her remarkable story in her book, *Secret Thoughts of an Unlikely Convert.*

She was a self-described "leftist lesbian professor" who despised Christians and frequently berated them in class. She was a tenured professor in English and women's studies at Syracuse University. She wrote frequently against Christians and the political tactics of the religious Right.

One article in particular gained lots of attention, most of it hate mail, but one letter from a Pastor Ken grabbed hold of her. She wanted to dismiss it but couldn't. She threw it away but then pulled it out of the trash. It challenged her assumptions in a way that she couldn't dismiss, but it was written with such kindness. She came to know the pastor, meeting with him and his wife. That meeting led to more meetings, and those meetings led to her reading the Bible. She writes:

> I continued reading the Bible, all the while fighting the idea that it was inspired. But the Bible got to be bigger inside me than I. It overflowed into my world. I fought against it with all my might. Then, one Sunday morning, I rose from the bed of my lesbian lover, and an hour later sat in a pew at the Syracuse Reformed Presbyterian Church. Conspicuous with my butch haircut, I reminded myself that I came to meet God, not fit in.
>
> I fought with everything I had.

I did not want this.

I did not ask for this.

I counted the costs. And I did not like the math on the other side of the equal sign.

But God's promises rolled in like sets of waves into my world . . . I was a thinker. I was paid to read books and write about them. I expected that in all areas of life, understanding came before obedience. I wanted to be the judge, not one being judged.

But the Scripture promised understanding after obedience. I wrestled with the question: Did I really want to understand homosexuality from God's point of view, or did I just want to argue with him? I prayed that night that God would give me the willingness to obey before I understood. I prayed long into the unfolding of day. When I looked in the mirror, I looked the same. But when I looked into my heart through the lens of the Bible, I wondered, Am I a lesbian, or has this all been a case of mistaken identity? If Jesus could split the world asunder, divide marrow from soul, could he make my true identity prevail?

Who am I? Who will God have me to be?

Then, one ordinary day, I came to Jesus, openhanded and naked. In this war of worldviews, Ken was there. The church that had been praying for me for years was there. Jesus triumphed. And I was a broken mess. Conversion was a train wreck. I did not want to lose everything that I loved. But the voice of God sang a sanguine love song in the rubble of my world. I weakly believed that if Jesus could conquer death, he could make right my world.

I have not forgotten the blood Jesus surrendered for this life.[2]

It is natural for us to fear what we will lose—but our fear is misdirected. We should be *more* afraid of missing what Jesus has for us, of forfeiting what is of eternal value. Let's consider not just what we're letting go of; let's also consider what we're taking hold of—Jesus himself. Following Jesus will not ultimately disappoint.

All to Him I Owe

The cross changes everything. We sing, "Jesus paid it all / All to him I owe."[3] Since Christ gave it all, something on our side also has to give. What do we need to release, to hand over, to offer up to him?

Jesus tells us: Deny yourself, take up your cross, and follow me. Only when we fix our eyes on Jesus will we see that it will cost us everything—and it's worth that price. C. S. Lewis says it well in his classic *Mere Christianity*:

But there must be a real giving up of the self. . . . The very first step is to try to forget about the self altogether. Your real, new self . . . will not come as long as you are looking for it. It will come when you are looking for him. . . . Keep back nothing. Nothing that you have not given away will ever be really yours. . . . Look for yourself, and you will find in the long run only hatred, loneliness, despair, rage, ruin, and decay. But look for Christ and you will find him, and with him everything else thrown in.[4]

When we look to Christ, we see that he has already done far more *for* us than he has asked *of* us.

- When we consider sacrificing money, let us look to Christ. He left all the riches of heaven to become a poor, homeless, traveling preacher—so that we could take hold of what is infinitely more valuable.

- When we consider loss of reputation or friends or popularity, let us look to Christ, whose closest friends abandoned him when he needed them most, whom the crowds cheered one day then crucified the next—so that we could be welcomed into the family of God.

- When we think of being made fun of, let us look to Christ, who was mocked, spat on, jeered at, though not a word of it was true—so that we could know the blessing and acceptance of the Father.

- When we think of physical suffering, even to the point of losing our lives, let us look to Christ, who was beaten, pierced, and executed as a common criminal, even though he didn't deserve it—so that we could be made whole!

Jesus willingly gave up everything because it was worth it. Jesus, who "for the joy set before him . . . endured the cross, scorning its shame" (Hebrews 12:2). Jesus did all that for you, for me, for us. He isn't asking us to do something that he hasn't already done for us; he even gives us the power to accomplish the task set before us.

"Look," Jesus says, "I gave all of me for all of you," and in return, how can we say anything but, "Jesus, I give you all of me for all of you!" It's worth it! There is no gap that cannot be bridged by the cross; there is no lifestyle, no belief system, no false religion, and no orientation that is beyond Jesus' reach.

Some of us have persisted in a casual, vampire Christianity, keeping Jesus at arm's length. Return to the King. Some of us are holding back, demanding more answers to our questions; Jesus has already given us plenty of answers and promises even more understanding on the other side of surrender. Return to the King. Some of us have professed faith in Jesus' words, but our hidden and secret actions show we are far from him. Repent and return to the King.

What do we need to leave? For some of us, there may be one big thing, while others of us may need to let go of lots of little things. If we've never left anything, we've never really followed. But Jesus sets the challenge even greater than that: if we're not willing to leave everything, we're not really following.

Here is the math. There is nothing you can give in exchange for your soul, and there is nothing better than what Jesus has promised. Let us look for Christ, surrender ourselves, take up our cross, and follow the King! There is no better place to be than surrendered to him.

CHAPTER 3

SCRIPTURE STUDY: Philippians 2:5-11 and Mark 8:34-35

Discussion Questions

1. What does it look like to live your life as though you are a sneak preview of "coming attractions"?

2. Which is harder, to surrender to God in the big things, or in the many little things throughout your life?

3. How do you know if you've reduced your faith to "vampire Christianity"?

4. What are you afraid of losing as you follow Jesus?

Further Reading: *The Secret Thoughts of an Unlikely Convert,* Rosaria Champagne Butterfield

WANT TO CHANGE THE WORLD?

FOUR

College students want to change the world. Walk around campus, and it's easy to see the incredible variety of causes to get behind. Fight sex trafficking. Save rain forests. Save whales. Save animals, period. Anti-Wall Street. Anti-texting. Anti-immigration. Pro-immigration. Pro-choice. Pro-life.

Some of these causes get tangled up in "slacktivism," where the involvement consists merely of pressing "Like" or buying a pair of TOMS shoes. (Hey, if I can look good and do good at the same time, that's a win-win.) But regardless of the level of engagement, all of this commotion speaks to a desire for change. Change is in the air and the water and everything else. College students are a cause-happy crowd, with good reason.

The world is a broken place, as most of us are well aware. It's impossible to ignore the pain, injustice, and evil in the world, without becoming callous. If we're not upset about something, we're simply not paying attention. If we're not fired up or fed up, we should have someone check our pulse. Or perhaps, check our focus. The more self-focused we are, the less we will know—or care—about the welfare of others. Wanting to see things change shows that we don't think life is all about me.

What do you care about? What breaks your heart? What tenses up your muscles, brings tears to your eyes, and puts passion in your voice? What are your areas of "holy discontent"? It's impossible to understand, let alone fix, everything. But what has God put on your heart? Out of all the broken things out there, what moves you?

Many of us know we want to change something, somehow, even if we don't know what it is. Steve Jobs, founder of Apple, famously said, "We're here to put a dent in the universe." We resonate with that sentiment. We want our lives to matter, to have significance.

So let's say we're successful. Let's say we change some things. What have we actually accomplished? When I talk with atheists or skeptics, we'll often get around to a cause they're passionate about. And I always ask, "Why do you care about that? What does it matter, if when we die we just slip into the abyss of oblivion?" For a Christian or non-Christian, where does this hunger, desire, and need for change come from?

Where does it come from? That's easy. God. "He has planted eternity in the human heart" (Ecclesiastes 3:11, NLT). Deep down, everyone knows—Christian and non-Christian alike—that this world is not what it is meant to be. It is not as God created it. It is wrong, twisted, corrupted, perverted, broken, and messed up. We know that—even creation itself knows that, as it groans for things to be made right again (Romans 8:22). What you want, whether or not you realize it, is for things—all things—to be made right. You desire peace—God's peace, his *shalom*—to rest on all things, transforming them into new creations. You want broken things to be made whole, captive people to be redeemed, warring factions to be reconciled.

The danger is not that you're too cause-driven but that you're not passionate *enough*. The danger is that you're diluting your energy on lots of tangential things, without connecting them to God's greater purposes. The danger is that you're not giving yourself to "The Cause"—the kingdom of God, which is the cause that literally ends all other causes. Do you want to change the world? Join up with the kingdom of God. It's the only cause guaranteed to succeed.

So how do we do that? How can we be a part of the change that the world—and we—so desperately need?

Change Starts with Us

People come up with some great ideas to change the world, but it would be a mistake to think that all we have to do is identify a need and jump right in. I've seen many people stall out or even crash and burn. There are always several reasons for burn out, but the biggest one is this: change starts with us and works from the inside out.

Imagine standing with Jesus and the disciples in Acts 1. Jesus has risen from the dead, and he's about to leave for heaven. He tells his confused and fearful followers that they "will be my witnesses in Jerusalem, and in all Judea and Samaria, and to the ends of the earth" (Acts 1:8). Jesus ascends into the clouds, and the disciples say, "Great speech. All right, let's go get 'em, boys!" They go out immediately, preaching, healing, and changing the world . . . right? Actually, that's not what happened.

It wasn't until the Holy Spirit came upon them in Acts 2 that they were filled with faith and power. Acts tells the story of how the good news continued to spread into Judea and Samaria and finally to the ends of the earth. That movement continued to snowball over the next decades and centuries until it covered the known world—just like Jesus said it would.

The Holy Spirit changes people, and changed people change the world. Before we seek global change, or cultural change, we must first be changed. It starts with us. Jesus makes this clear when he tells his disciples, "Peace be with you! As the Father has sent me, I am sending you" (John 20:21). First, Jesus gives us his peace, his *shalom*—the source of redemption of all things that we long for. That peace changes us. Then (and only then), he sends us out into the world, in the same way that the Father sent him.

The first change—when sin came into the world—worked from the inside out as well. It produced alienation between humans and God, within our own selves, between us and other humans, and between humans and creation. So redemption works the same way. It reconciles us to God, ourselves, each other, and the world.

The change we seek has to start somewhere. It starts with us and then flows outward. This is why we have to bow the knee first, declaring Jesus as King. You can't be an agent of the kingdom unless you have surrendered to the King. The inside-out change, which begins in us, has two dimensions. The same gospel that changes us also transforms the world. These are not two different things—they are two different ways of telling the same story. I like how Matt Chandler talks about this in his book *The Explicit Gospel*.[1] He talks about "The Gospel on the Ground" and "The Gospel in the Air."

The Gospel on the Ground

The gospel on the ground is the story of salvation that most of us are familiar with. It is the story of personal salvation. It explains that we are created in the image of God but that, because of sin, we are fallen and separated from God. "For all have sinned and fall short of the glory of God" (Romans 3:23). Left to ourselves in sin, we are without God and without hope in this world. We are by nature objects of wrath, justly deserving God's punishment for our sins and offenses against him. We cannot save ourselves. No matter how hard we try. No matter how much good we do. No matter how many causes we volunteer for or give money to. "There is no one who does good, not even one" (Romans 3:12). The chasm created by sin is a gap that none of us can bridge, no matter how hard we try.

One of my favorite ways of describing this to an unbeliever is to take an imaginary trip to the Grand Canyon. I say, "Imagine that you, me, and the Olympic gold medalist in the long jump stood on the edge of the Grand Canyon. We were commanded to jump. I jumped, and it was pathetic. You went next, and because you have better hops than me, you got farther out—but still nowhere near the other side. Then the gold medalist went. He got a lot farther than either of us—but still landed miles away from the other side." Then we discuss how this represents what all of our efforts to save ourselves ultimately lead to, no matter how "good" we are. We need a bridge, which is exactly what this familiar illustration depicts.

The gospel on the ground explodes every other self-salvation strategy that we come up with. All attempts to make ourselves right—whether through religion, being a good person, or saving the world through our cause of choice—fall far short. Jesus did for us what we could not do for ourselves. And because of him, our guilt is forgiven. We are declared righteous. Our shame is removed. We are washed and cleansed. We are being made holy, made to be like Christ. We are adopted into the family of God. We are born again, from within, by the Holy Spirit. We have a new identity, a new nature, and a new destiny. Knowing and believing these things should bring great freedom and joy to us. You can't be a Christian without affirming your personal need for Jesus Christ. If your faith isn't personal, that is, if Jesus didn't die and rise again for you, then it's no faith at all.

The Gospel in the Air

But the gospel on the ground isn't the whole story. There's a big story being written, of which our individual stories are a part. While human beings are unique among God's creation, and placed as stewards over it, we are not all that God has created. God's kingdom is concerned with us and our hearts, but it is also concerned with much more than just us. God has a plan of redemption that includes all creation. To have a God-sized view of his redemptive plan, we need to see that God wants to restore *all things* to his original design. God has a plan, and we get to be a part of that. To paraphrase Shakespeare, the whole world is the stage, and we are just supporting actors in this grand drama. It's the story of "all things new," in which God redeems, restores, and reclaims what rightfully belongs to him, through Jesus Christ. Paul summarizes this well in his letter to the Colossians:

> He is the image of the invisible God, the firstborn of all creation. For by him all things were created, in heaven and on earth, visible and invisible, whether thrones or dominions or rulers or authorities—all things were created through him and for him. And he is before all things, and in him all things hold together. And he is the head of the body, the church. He is the beginning, the firstborn from the dead, that in everything he might be preeminent. For in him all the fullness of God was pleased to dwell, and through him to reconcile to himself all things, whether on earth or in heaven, making peace by the blood of his cross. (Colossians 1:15-20, ESV)

This drama has four acts: Creation, Fall, Redemption, and Consummation.

1. **Creation.** God created the world and everything in it, and it was good. Everything belongs to him. Everything was created to give God glory and pleasure. There was no sin or imperfection in God's original creation. "Worthy are you, our Lord and God, to receive glory and honor and power, for you created all things, and by your will they existed and were created" (Revelation 4:11, ESV).

2. **Fall.** But sin came into the world through the agency of Satan and the original sin of Adam and Eve. This sin has corrupted, twisted, stained, and perverted everything. So while we can still see God's handiwork around us, it is far from what he designed. It separates us from him, and it is fatal. It is like a drop of lethal poison in a glass of water. And we've all drunk from that cup. We are both victims and perpetrators of sin, which is the source of all pain, hurt, war, famine, crime, violence, and everything else dark in this world.

3. **Redemption.** Scripture doesn't tell us why evil came into the world, but it does tell us what God is doing about it. Jesus does for humans (and all creation) what we could not do for ourselves. He lives a perfect life and fulfills God's righteous requirements. Though he is sinless, he becomes sin for us. Jesus conquers sin through his atoning death on the cross, dying the death we should have died, in our place. He conquers death through his resurrection. Jesus is uniquely able to save the world, because

he is both fully God and fully human. His victory over sin and death unleashes resurrection power, the definitive moment in which his new kingdom begins its advance. Things will never be the same. They are at this moment being made right. Our full redemption is already here—but not yet all the way here.

4. **Consummation**. This story has an ending. Things are not going to be looped on repeat forever. One day Jesus will return and heaven will descend to earth. Evil and all its forces will be definitively defeated. All results of evil will be wiped away. All things will finally be made right. "Behold, I am making all things new" (Revelation 21:5, ESV). God will dwell with his people, and we will exist with him forever, in perfect joy and intimacy.

It's important to note that we need both stories, both dimensions of the gospel (ground and air), to fully understand who Jesus is and what he is King over. The gospel on the ground tells us who we are, what's wrong with us, and what God can do for us. The gospel in the air tells us it's not about us but about him and his bigger plan. It also tells us that everything matters. Jesus is reconciling all things to himself. If all things matter to him, they should matter to us. Everything, then, is "spiritual." Everything can become a means to worship God, if we approach it that way. "Your kingdom is an everlasting kingdom, and your dominion endures throughout all generations. The LORD is faithful in all his words and kind in all his works" (Psalm 145:13, ESV).

Faithful Engagement

The combination of the personal story and the big story has profound implications for how you approach your life, and your desire to change your campus—and even the world. The gospel on the ground tells us that changed people change the world. Transformation starts with us. The gospel in the air tells us that we are part of God's big story and everything matters. Transformation's goal is nothing less than all things.

If we're talking about all things, where on earth do we begin? Let's start with what's in front of us, one day at a time, in the places where God has already located us. Let that inside-out change flow from you and out to all the people and places you touch every day. Let's take your relationship with your roommate. The gospel on the ground says your roommate is a sinner whose greatest need is Jesus. You should be looking for ways to share the gospel with him or her. Telling your roommate about Jesus is the best thing you can do for him or her.

The kingdom of God expands as one person shares the good news with another. The gospel on the ground also tells you that *you* are a sinner who needs Jesus. Are you humbled by that? Are you gracious with your roommate's mistakes, because you know how many you make? Do you choose to overlook small offenses and forgive bigger ones? Do you ask for forgiveness and look for ways to point to Jesus in your successes and in your failures?

But we're not done. The kingdom of God goes forward in other ways. The gospel in the air is about connecting our stories to the big stories, and about how everything takes on eternal significance. So all the ways you treat your roommate—whether or not you're sharing the gospel at that moment—take on meaning. Jesus even said that giving a child a cup of cold water because we're his disciples would be rewarded in heaven (Matthew 10:42). So being patient when your roommate's alarm goes off for the fifteenth time, instead of irritated, pleases God. Picking up your roommate's stuff or doing his or her dishes pleases God. Not being aloof or cold when you're tired and would rather go to bed pleases God. It all matters.

We could say much more about other areas, such as the way you do your classwork and interact with professors and peers. Or the way you handle romantic and family relationships. There's not an area in your life where Jesus can't or shouldn't come in. In the kingdom of God, every moment is infused with an "eternal weight of glory" (2 Corinthians 4:17, ESV), which C. S. Lewis so memorably wrote about.[2]

Kingdom people are conscious of this and seek what I call *faithful engagement*.[3] Faithful engagement is an attitude. It views everything through the lens of faith, and asks, "What would this look like if it was fully surrendered to Jesus, if it was fully redeemed by Jesus?" By "faithful," I mean the intentional posture of being true to Jesus' commands. We're his subjects and want to do what he says. By "engagement," I mean active involvement in the world around us. On one hand, that means not fearfully retreating into "holy huddles" where everyone thinks and looks and acts exactly like us, in order to be "safe." Jesus specifically said he would not pray for us to do that: "I do not ask that you take them out of the world, but that you keep them from the evil one" (John 17:15, ESV).

On the other hand, faithful engagement doesn't mean going on a power trip. It doesn't mean Jesus' victory will come through military might, violence, political power, or other this-world strategies. Jesus made this clear when he told Pilate: "My kingdom is not of this world. If my kingdom were of this world, my servants would have been fighting, that I might not be delivered over to the Jews. But my kingdom is not from the world" (John 18:36, ESV). Surely, we've seen Christians make both mistakes. Some are too passive, fearful, and removed from the world to make any eternal difference. This grieves Jesus. Others are too aggressive, and their strategies of force don't lead to Jesus being any more loved or worshiped—quite the opposite, in fact.

Faithful engagement is a third, less obvious, way. Fortunately we have an example in the Bible. Remember our friends in Babel, mentioned in chapter 1? When we left them, they were trying to build a tower to make a name for themselves, and God scattered them. Well, eventually those people gathered again, and built a great empire—the Babylonian empire. It was so great that it conquered the known world, contributed an ancient wonder of the world with its hanging gardens, and generally wreaked havoc. Babylon was so wicked that it became a symbol of all that is wrong in the world, so much so that in Revelation, the "whore of Babylon" is one of the biggest villains.

Babylon's evil ambitions eventually extended to Judah, where they raped, pillaged, and took away the Jews' best and brightest, including some guys you may have heard of, like Daniel, Shadrach, Meshach, and Abednego. Put yourself in their shoes. You're young, smart, and God-fearing, living in the capital of the empire that killed your family, destroyed your temple, and hates your God. Everything around you tries to seduce you into your captor's way of life, but you're trying to remain faithful to God. How would you live? What would you do? Give in and hope for the best? Or maybe start a revolution, plot some domestic terrorism? The young guys receive a letter from the prophet Jeremiah, with a message from God.

Amazingly, God doesn't say, "Burn the city! I will have my vengeance!" Rather, God's instructions for the captives are:

This is what the LORD Almighty, the God of Israel, says to all those I carried into exile from Jerusalem to Babylon: "Build houses and settle down; plant gardens and eat what they produce. Marry and have sons and daughters; find wives for your sons and give your daughters in marriage, so that they too may have sons and daughters. Increase in number there; do not decrease. Also, seek the peace and prosperity of the city to which I have carried you into exile. Pray to the LORD for it, because if it prospers, you too will prosper." (Jeremiah 29:4-7)

I don't know about you, but if I had received this letter, I would have checked the return address. "Peace and prosperity? Pray for it—for the Babylonians, God? You're connecting my prosperity to theirs? No way!" Not only that, but God tells them to build houses, get married, have kids, and settle down. "As long as you're there, leave a legacy, do some good, do some things that will bless long after you're gone." In other words, "Do some kingdom good, because making things better and more beautiful pleases me."

What about your campus? Its godlessness may rival Babylon's. You may be both repulsed and tempted by the things you see around you. But God is calling you to faithful engagement with it. What if your greatest accomplishment during college isn't what you take with you—diploma, killer resume, job offer—but what you leave behind? What if the best thing you could say about your college career is that you left a campus better than you found it, a place where the kingdom has come, a place where God's *shalom* flourishes? May God give us holy imaginations to dream about what that could look like.

Let's Start a Movement

But how can we start a movement? And why can we have confidence that it will accomplish much?

Because Jesus is King. We know where history is headed, and it ends with him on the throne, reconciling all things to himself. "Behold, I am making all things new" (Revelation 21:5, ESV). He promises all this, and we can claim these promises, because "the one who calls you is faithful, and he will do it" (1 Thessalonians 5:24).

The kingdom of God is on the move. So let's join the movement, a movement of the King, a people who are transformed and transforming the world.

CHAPTER 4

SCRIPTURE STUDY: Colossians 1:15-20; Jeremiah 29:4-14

Discussion Questions

1. What kind of change do you want to see in the world? Why?

2. "Change starts with us and works from the inside out." Do you agree, and why is this important?

3. Which dimension of the gospel story—"on the ground" or "in the air"—are you more familiar with? What is the importance of witnessing to both?

4. In what ways is God calling you to pray and seek the peace and prosperity of your campus?

FIVE

HOLY AND WHOLE

How Do I Get Clean?

I had a college roommate who was a bit of a germaphobe. He regularly asked a philosophical question about the nature of soap: "If we use soap to get clean, then how does soap get *itself* clean?" Despite its metaphysical implications, he usually asked this question in frustration, after finding out that one of the other roommates had used his soap. Our typical response? "I don't know, it's soap. That's what it does. Just use it!" Of course, we said this with complete compassion, understanding, and empathy. He didn't like that answer, though, so he always threw away his soap if anybody else used it.

Fear of germs may not be your thing, but increasingly, it is common for people to be fearful or anxious about something. Many of us walk around with various disorders (whether or not diagnosed), such as panic disorder, post-traumatic stress disorder (PTSD), generalized anxiety disorder, obsessive-compulsive disorder (OCD—or as my slightly OCD friend puts it, "CDO, because then the letters are in the proper order"), social phobia, agoraphobia (fear of public places), and many more.

I interact with a lot of hurting people. It's part of my job. But you interact with them too. Fearful, wounded, damaged, hurting people surround us. They are us. Not surprisingly, many people have a strong desire to find help and healing. When I begin meeting one-on-one with students, that's usually what they are hoping our meetings will accomplish. They want to gather all the wounded fragments of themselves and be put together again. They long to be made whole.

As much as I hear that people long for wholeness, I hear very little concern for holiness. Those two things are far more than words that sound sort-of similar. They are deeply connected. I don't think it's a coincidence that the more our culture turns away from God's standards for how we should live, the more we become anxious, fearful, self-centered, and despairing. The question people are asking is: "How do I get myself clean?" That's more than philosophical, and it's more urgent than soap. How can we become whole?

As amazing as God has made us, and as incredible as life can be, we know that we are not yet what we could be or should be. We are not yet fully human. Sin prevents us from being fully human or whole; holiness is God's design for us to become what he has created us to be, apart from sin. The path to wholeness goes through holiness. Do you want to become fully human? Become like Jesus.

Therefore, with minds that are alert and fully sober, set your hope on the grace to be brought to you when Jesus Christ is revealed at his coming. As obedient children, do not conform to the evil desires you had when you lived in ignorance. But just as he who called you is holy, so be holy in all you do; for it is written: "Be holy, because I am holy." (1 Peter 1:13-16)

God says to "be holy, because I am holy." Yet I know I probably have a tough sell to convince you of this. As R. C. Sproul wrote:

We tend to have mixed feelings about the holy. There is a sense in which we are at the same time attracted to it and repulsed by it. Something draws us toward it, while at the same time we want to run away from it. We can't seem to decide which way we want it. Part of us yearns for the holy, while part of us despises it. We can't live with it, and we can't live without it.[1]

I'm Not Into Your Traditional Values

If we're halfhearted about holiness, our culture often seems wholeheartedly against it. The stories being told on our campuses basically say that to live biblically is traditional and outdated. If you're progressive and thoughtful, then you'll move away from that old-fashioned morality and get with the times. What's ironic is that behaviors like getting drunk, living as if you'll die tomorrow, and sleeping around are just as old-fashioned. There's nothing new or progressive about them. Biblical values aren't traditional (stodgy)—they're timeless and radical. If anything, it's the pagan stuff that is old and tired—and destructive. When biblical holiness was introduced to the Gentiles in the New Testament (especially in places like Corinth), they were ridiculous and newfangled. Paul had to tell them, "Here's an idea: don't encourage anyone to sleep with his step-mom. And certainly don't celebrate it!" I'm sure the Corinthian "traditionalists" shook their heads at Paul's crazy advice. Living biblically has never been easy.

Under the banner of tolerance, even many Christians have embraced a live-and-let-live philosophy. It seems loving and compassionate. But it actually shows a lack of concern and even apathy for what is right and good. I like how Dorothy L. Sayers put it: "In the world it calls itself Tolerance; but in Hell it is called Despair . . . the sin that believes in nothing, cares for nothing, seeks to know nothing, interferes with nothing, enjoys nothing, loves nothing, hates nothing, finds purpose in nothing, lives for nothing, and only remains alive because there is nothing it would die for."[2]

If we're honest, we're more influenced by current social practices than we'd like to admit. We don't want to seem pathetic, so even if we don't do the "really bad" stuff that everyone else is doing, we'll let some things slide. I see Christian students tolerating and even celebrating things that have no place among God's people, like excessive sexual involvement with others (whether in boyfriend/girlfriend relationships or just hooking up), drinking and even getting drunk, and viewing websites and movies that are impure and certainly unhelpful (even if they're not quite pornographic). One ministry I know surveyed their students and asked them about viewing porn. I'll give it to these students: they were honest. 100 percent of the guys and 60 percent of the girls who completed the survey said that they had watched porn in the last few months.

We are far too comfortable with sin. One reason for this is that we play the comparison game.

- "At least what I'm doing isn't as bad as _____ (fill in the blank)."
- "At least I'm only looking at people having sex, not having it myself."
- "At least I'm having sex in a loving, committed relationship, not sleeping around."
- "At least I'm only having a few drinks, not getting totally wasted."
- "At least I only cheat in this one class, not all of them like some people."

I told you this book wouldn't be about beer and sex, and it isn't. But we need to talk about it, because we need to talk about holiness and God's design for our lives. We need to hate sin. The best thing for us is to run from it. But here's how insidious it is: the more empty and fragmented (nonwhole) we feel, the more we run into it. We run to sinful coping mechanisms instead of God himself. The girl who doesn't feel quite lovely or beautiful enough will cram herself into some tight-fitting clothes, drink too much alcohol, and throw herself at several guys, hoping one of them will make her feel loved and significant and desirable, even if for only one night. But she doesn't need a guy if she knows who she is in God's eyes.

The problem with the comparison game of "At least I'm better than . . ." is that it's a dead-end. God blows that up by declaring, "Be holy, because I am holy." The only standard that matters is God's. And if we're measuring against that, we see how much we need God. That's the point.

What Is Holiness, Really?

Huge volumes of theology have been written on the subject of holiness; so let me acknowledge that this summary is vastly incomplete. But we can at least start to understand holiness in the following ways.

God Is Holy

To know what holiness is, and why it matters, we have to look at God. What do the angels sing about in heaven? Holiness. "Holy, holy, holy" (Revelation 4:8). To say that God is holy (the Greek word *agios*) is to say that he is utterly different, that he is *Other*, that he is set apart. Holiness is an essential aspect of God's character. It means that he is worthy of all worship and deserving of all honor. There's nothing good that he doesn't deserve. It also means that he is pure, sinless, and upright. There is something frightening about this completely sinless Other, and it's not just "the Old Testament God." We do see the ancient Israelites shaking in their boots as they stand at the foot of the thundering Mount Sinai. But we also see Peter, when he realizes that Jesus is holy, saying, "Go away from me, Lord; I am a sinful man!" (Luke 5:8). The modern desire to say, "God is love," and stop there is not new. People have been trying to put the God of the Universe in a box forever. J. C. Ryle warns us about this:

> Beware of manufacturing a God of your own—a God who is all mercy but not just,—a God who is all love, but not holy,—a God who has a heaven for everybody, but a hell for none,—a God who can allow good and bad to be side by side in time, but will make no distinction between good and bad in eternity. Such a God is an idol of your own . . . as true an idol as any snake or crocodile in an Egyptian temple . . . The hands of your own fancy and sentimentality have made Him. He is not the God of the Bible, and beside the God of the Bible there is no God at all.[3]

We Must Be Holy

Because God is holy, God's people must be holy. It's a mark or a sign of the kingdom. Holiness is meant to be central to who we are. "Be holy, because I am holy." That's not a suggestion; that's a command. So to truly reflect the image of God, we must reflect his holiness. Holiness is about being different, about being set apart or consecrated for God's purposes.

Not only that, but holiness is essential to our relationship with God. "Make every effort to live in peace with everyone and to be holy; without holiness no one will see the Lord" (Hebrews 12:14). Are you frustrated in your relationship with God, wondering why he sometimes seems distant? There may be something in your life that you are tolerating, but God does not. Those acceptable sins become giant walls or blinders that keep us from seeing God. In repentance, we turn away from those things and turn to God. Without holiness, no one can see the Lord. But with holiness, we can and we will.

Holiness, as God's standard, is also how we become closer to one another. I love how A. W. Tozer helps us picture this:

Has it ever occurred to you that one hundred pianos all tuned to the same fork are automatically tuned to each other? They are of one accord by being tuned, not to each other, but to another standard to which each one must individually bow. So one hundred worshipers met together, each one looking away to Christ, are in heart nearer to each other than they could possibly be were they to become "unity" conscious and turn their eyes away from God to strive for closer fellowship.[4]

Holiness Is Becoming Who We Are in Christ

Holiness comes through union with Christ, through our connection to him. Holiness is the result of the gospel, the good news of the kingdom. The author of Hebrews writes, "For by one sacrifice he has made perfect forever those who are being made holy" (Hebrews 10:14). Through Jesus and his work for us on the cross, we are declared righteous. We have already been made perfect in God's eyes, and we are being progressively made holy in this life. So in that sense, holiness is becoming who you already are in Christ. In other words, this holiness is not only for God but also by God. It's through his grace. It's by Jesus' one-time sacrifice, not any sacrifice of yours.

This is really good news for those of us who know we are far from holy, or whole. Graceless religion and try-harder moralism would leave us high and dry. Religion says, "You have to clean your act up to be accepted, and if you're too screwed up, too bad." But the gospel says, "You are accepted. And God gives you the grace to be cleaned up. There is no one who cannot be made holy or be made whole." The difference between religion and the gospel is indescribably vast.

The gospel says that in Christ, you and I have been redeemed by something of enduring, imperishable worth: Jesus' blood. We were born again, with imperishable worth, through the word of God. God declares us to be infinitely worthy, valuable, beautiful, and priceless to him. You are God's priceless work of art. This should be all the worth any of us needs.

Holiness Showcases the Gospel

Because of the gospel, holiness isn't the harsh moralism of "clean up your act, or else!" Instead, holiness calls us to "start acting like what you are, what God has made you to be!" The gospel is a jewel of incalculable worth. You now have that jewel. If you want to showcase the gospel, what do you surround it with? Have you ever been to a jewelry store? When you shop for a diamond, the whole store is beautiful—clean, immaculate, and classy. Then they bring out the diamonds. They place them on black velvet, under sharp, powerful spotlights designed to bring out every facet of the jewel. As they talk about the four Cs, they carefully move the diamond back and forth under the light, causing the sparkle to jump out at you. Now that's how you show off a jewel.

I suppose you could look at the same jewels in a dumpy place, like a dingy old Laundromat. The fluorescent lights flicker in the background as some people argue across the room. A shady character uses his grubby hands to put the jewels on a grimy plastic table. Those diamonds could be just as good as the ones you saw in the jewelry store—but how would you know? Which place would you buy a ring from?

Friends, the gospel is the jewel. Holiness is the setting. Holiness is crucial to the kingdom, because by it we show off what is good, true, righteous, beautiful, admirable, excellent, and awesome about the gospel.

Holiness Is About Purity

There's no ignoring the fact that the Bible forbids certain things. Some things do not belong in the kingdom of God—they belong to another kingdom. This includes many things that are common and celebrated on college campuses:

Now the works of the flesh are evident: sexual immorality, impurity, sensuality, idolatry, sorcery, enmity, strife, jealousy, fits of anger, rivalries, dissensions, divisions, envy, drunkenness, orgies, and things like these. I warn you, as I warned you before, that those who do such things will not inherit the kingdom of God. (Galatians 5:19-21, ESV)

Paul continues, contrasting these works with the more familiar fruit of the Spirit:

But the fruit of the Spirit is love, joy, peace, patience, kindness, goodness, faithfulness, gentleness, self-control; against such things there is no law. And those who belong to Christ Jesus have crucified the flesh with its passions and desires. If we live by the Spirit, let us also walk with the Spirit. (Galatians 5:22-25, ESV)

Holiness is about turning away from the "works of the flesh." By putting to death our sinful nature, and living by the Holy Spirit, we bear good fruit. The call for a Christian is to be holy and pure. "Since we have these promises, beloved, let us cleanse ourselves from every defilement of body and spirit, bringing holiness to completion in the fear of God" (2 Corinthians 7:1, ESV).

Holiness is not only doing what God wants us to do but also thinking like him. Holiness is the habit of being of one mind with God, as we find his mind described in Scripture. It is the habit of agreeing in God's judgment—hating what he hates, loving what he loves, and measuring everything in this world by the standard of his Word.[5]

Holiness Is Not Legalism

I'm sure some of you have already been thinking, "Oh great. I think I smell some legalism here. Yet another attempt to control people through rules and religion, instead of leading them to a life-giving relationship." That's a serious charge—and definitely not good news. But thankfully, that's not what a call to true holiness is.

Holiness is not legalism. Obedience is not legalism. It seems many people's working definition of legalism is "being told to do something I don't want to do." That's not legalism. Legalism is the attempt to earn God's favor through keeping a set of rules. It's about external conformity and looking good, without a genuine inside-out heart change. It's the religion of the Pharisees and the moralists. Legalists act like they're on God's team (and think that God's lucky to have them). But their actions show that they don't love God (they love looking good), and they don't trust God (they trust themselves to save themselves). Two people might do the exact same thing, like feed the homeless. The legalist does it hoping that God or others will notice how great he is. He's adding to his "good column." But the Christian rests on her identity in Christ. She doesn't need to add to any righteousness column; she simply serves out of love for God and others. If no one notices, that's OK. She's simply obeying, out of love.

> We know that we have come to know him if we obey his commands. Whoever says, "I know him," but does not do what he commands is a liar, and the truth is not in that person. But if anyone obeys his word, love for God is truly made complete in them. This is how we know we are in him: Whoever claims to live in him must live as Jesus did. (1 John 2:3-6)

Holiness loves obedience. It isn't a slave to the Law, but it doesn't throw off all restraints either. It celebrates the positive restraints given through God's law. I hear people say all the time that "I don't want a system of rules—that's religion. I'm all about having a relationship." That sounds good, until you ask, "How should I live in this relationship?" I have a relationship with my wife. When we got married, we exchanged vows of what we promised to do (and not do) for each other. Things like caring for each other no matter what, and forsaking all others. Those "rules" haven't gotten in the way of our relationship; they've directed and deepened it. It's the same way with God's rules. His commands show us how to have a relationship with him. That's not legalism—that's love. As Kevin DeYoung says:

> It sounds really spiritual to say God is interested in a relationship, not in rules. But it's not biblical. From top to bottom, the Bible is full of commands. They aren't meant to stifle a relationship with God, but to protect it, seal it, and define it. Never forget: first God delivered the Israelites from Egypt, then He gave them the law. God's people were not redeemed by observing the law. But they were redeemed so that they might obey the law.[6]

You Want Holiness

Don't be afraid of all this holiness talk. Some of us struggle with the call to be holy, thinking it is too antiquated, too religious. But let me demonstrate that we have a desire for holiness, even if we don't call it that. Let's use Martin Luther King Jr. as an example. We celebrate MLK's contributions to civil rights, to furthering the proposition that all men are created equal and should be treated that way. But underneath this celebration is the fact that many people, still, are not treated equally. So, as a society, we have this secular holiday (or *holy* day) to remind ourselves: "Hey, we should keep striving to be cleansed from racial sins; and if our motives aren't pure toward people of other races, we should come clean." That's racial holiness.

We see similar motives in something like environmentalism. Do you get irritated when people don't recycle? Then you want them to be environmentally holy. We could say the same thing about most of the other causes that we care so deeply about: clean water, third world debt, access to AIDS drugs—these are generally agreed upon standards of public holiness. We just don't call it that.

Maybe we should call it true religion? After all, James writes, "Religion that is pure and undefiled before God, the Father, is this: to visit orphans and widows in their affliction, and to keep oneself unstained from the world" (James 1:27, ESV). See that? James defines true, holy (pure and undefiled) religion as standing before God, caring for the poor and needy, and being morally unstained.

Even unbelievers have an unconscious desire for holiness. They want people to want what is right, and to do it. But where did that sense of right and wrong come from? And how can we arrive at any meaningful definition of right and wrong? They don't make a whole lot of sense if there isn't some standard of holiness from God—a God who ultimately defines and decides what is right and wrong. People want holiness—even if they don't call it that and they don't want the God who defines it.

We readily associate concern for the poor with the kingdom of God. So why don't we also see personal holiness and wholeness as a sign of the kingdom? Jesus tied public and personal holiness together, saying, "But seek first the kingdom of God and his righteousness, and all these things will be added to you" (Matthew 6:33, ESV). The kingdom and "things made right" are tied together with righteousness and "us made right." In other words, God tells us, "Make it your first priority to seek the kingdom and the holiness I bring, and I'll take care of the rest."

This talk of holiness, far from being antiquated and annoying, actually speaks to a deep, deep longing in each of us. We long to be made whole, made right, to become once and for all released from the imperfections and limitations we feel. But if we seek first the kingdom of God and his righteousness, we will become truly, perfectly, fully human.

Holy Counterculture

Once you were not a people, but now you are the people of God; once you had not received mercy, but now you have received mercy. Dear friends, I urge you, as foreigners and exiles, to abstain from sinful desires, which wage war against your soul. Live such good lives among the pagans that, though they accuse you of doing wrong, they may see your good deeds and glorify God on the day he visits us. (1 Peter 2:10-12)

One reason we don't have a greater impact on our campuses is that we don't live as a holy counterculture, as foreigners and exiles, as citizens of another King and kingdom. Personal and public holiness is a sign that the kingdom is coming, and that allegiance is owed to another, better King. We ought to be different from "the world."

"The world" is not another way of saying "the people around us." The world is everything that opposes the will of God. To put it another way, worldliness is whatever makes sin look normal and righteousness look strange. In every society there is a principle of Babylon that makes war against the children of God.[7] To put it the other way around, then, holiness is whatever makes sin look strange and righteousness look normal. You can't do that on your own. That takes a community, on mission together. That takes a holy counterculture.

The kingdom of God will not move ahead if we do not demonstrate holiness with our lives. We show our allegiance to King Jesus by abstaining from sinful desires and committing to good deeds—like clean water, urban renewal, or any number of other just causes. In that, we are noticeably different from the world around us.

That's not to say that this counterculture can't be attractive. It will certainly be different. It will be mocked and made fun of. But a steadfast purity and rightness will speak to the echo of God's design in everyone, and some will be moved to listen. The more we are committed to personal and public holiness, the more we will be a distinct and compelling alternative to the world around us. We have something life-changing and life-giving to hold out to people. Let's show them that, in Christ, holiness leads to wholeness.

CHAPTER 5

SCRIPTURE STUDY: 1 Peter 1:13-16; Galatians 5:19-25

Discussion Questions

1. What do holiness and wholeness have in common? How are they related?

2. Christ says that he has made us holy, set apart. Do you believe you are holy? What might change for you if you began to trust that God has already fully redeemed you and accepts you as his beloved child?

3. How has God's holiness been portrayed to you throughout your life? Do you feel attracted to it, repulsed by it, or both? Discuss.

4. What's the difference between holiness and legalism? Which are you living into?

5. What does it mean to be countercultural and holy where you are today?

SIX KINGDOM PRAYER

Way back in 1806, five Williams College students—Samuel J. Mills, James Richards, Francis L. Robbins, Harvey Loomis, and Byram Green—gathered to pray for the realization of Jesus' command to go to all the nations, and China in particular. Classmates mocked them for their devout faith, and they had trouble finding a space on campus to meet. Looking for a secluded place to pray, they ventured out into a field. A sudden thunderstorm kicked up, but the only "shelter" they could find was in a haystack. Now I have to be honest—at this point, I'm probably throwing in the towel. Even the weather is conspiring against them. A lot of us would have quit, but not these five young men. The rain dampened the hay, but not their prayers, and the Haystack Prayer Meeting began. A change came over their campus, and many of the same classmates who had mocked them came to faith in Jesus and joined their prayer times.

This prayer meeting eventually ignited a movement to send generations of students into missions. The site of that little haystack became known as "the birthplace of American Foreign Missions," and eighty years later, deeply impacted men like John Mott and Luther Wishard. These two spearheaded the Student Volunteer Movement, which mobilized over one hundred thousand college students to spend their lives in foreign missions. All five of those Williams College men went into ministry. Their legacy lives on in countless missions organizations, including many campus ministries. Yes, there was a time when college students were leading the way in prayer and ministry. My prayer is that it will be that way again.

The problem with telling a two hundred-year-old story is that it doesn't seem relevant. But we should remember how central prayer is to the expansion of the kingdom of God. "When we work, we work. When we pray, God works." Those were the words of Hudson Taylor, the great missionary to China whose work was bathed in prayer—and as a result was able to see many people come to faith. It's the same on our campuses today. It's the same throughout church history and around the world. You simply can't find a great movement of God that does not start with prayer. In fact, many of the great movements of God have started when college students gathered to do nothing more than pray for their campuses and the world.

In my ministry, we've seen God work repeatedly in response to prayer. Recently, we realized that a good number of people hanging around our ministry were interested in following Christ, but not quite committing. So we put their names on a whiteboard and committed to praying for them daily. This was in addition to some other rhythms of prayer we were building into our ministry. In the last few months, we saw half of the people on that list make a commitment to Jesus. Does God hear prayer? The answer is an unequivocal yes.

Does God Hear Prayer?

I find that many of us have a mental block when it comes to prayer. Let's not wrap ourselves up in speculations, ignoring his clear promises in Scripture. Even if we mentally understand, it can be harder to convince our hearts. So here are some reasons that I hope will encourage you in your prayers.[1]

1. God identifies himself as the one who hears prayer (Psalm 65:2). As a God of infinite grace and mercy, he loves to answer the prayers of the needy. "The LORD is near to all who call on him, to all who call on him in truth" (Psalm 145:18). It's part of his nature.

2. God accepts our prayers as the requests of children to their father, and he is ready to act in response to them. "If you then, who are evil, know how to give good gifts to your children, how much more will your Father who is in heaven give good things to those who ask him!" (Matthew 7:11, ESV).

3. God has given us access to the throne of grace, through Jesus, at all times. "Let us then approach God's throne of grace with confidence, so that we may receive mercy and find grace to help us in our time of need" (Hebrews 4:16).

4. God encourages us to give him no rest from our prayers. He desires bold and forceful requests, where we won't let go until he blesses us (Luke 18:1-8).

5. God is ready to hear and answer our prayers. He takes notice of our prayers. "Before they call I will answer; while they are still speaking I will hear" (Isaiah 65:24).

6. God gives generously in response to our prayers, not according to what we deserve (James 1:5-6). He often gives "more than all we ask or imagine" (Ephesians 3:20-21).

7. The Bible is filled with stories of God doing great things in response to prayer. He delivers Moses and the Israelites from slavery in Egypt; he makes the sun stand still for Joshua; he makes the rain stop for three years for Elijah; he saves Hezekiah's life; he rescues the needy, releases people from prison, defeats enemies with his angel armies, and gives barren women children.

8. God hears us because of Jesus. Jesus is the (only) "mediator between God and humanity" (1 Timothy 2:5, HCSB). Jesus has paid for our sins with his blood, removing the guilt, which would divide us from God. Our prayers are also acceptable because of Jesus' perfection, which now counts for us. And even now, "Christ Jesus who died—more than that, who was raised to life—is at the right hand of God and is also interceding for us" (Romans 8:34).

But Why Prayer?

Why does God choose to work in response to prayer? Couldn't he work another way? He has good reasons.

First, prayer glorifies God. Prayer acknowledges our dependence on God. This active, conscious dependence gives him pleasure and praise. It pays him the honor he deserves as the author of life, the source of strength, and the giver of all good things. Prayer reminds us who the King is. He is the only one who truly understands, who is always there. Why do we spend so much time tweeting, posting, chatting, and blogging about our problems, instead of praying about them? Why do you talk with others, even your parents, your best friend, your counselor, or random strangers and neglect the most sympathetic and powerful ear? Their ability to comfort is secondary, and like the moon, any light they can shed on the subject is only a reflection. Go to the sun, to the "throne of grace," where you have the Almighty Father, an interceding Son, and the Holy Spirit—the indwelling Comforter herself.

Second, prayer works on us. It prepares us to receive God's mercy. The more we pray, the more it prepares us to receive his gifts. It reminds us how needy we are apart from him. It draws us into closer relationship with him and grows our desire for him. Prayer forces us to acknowledge that the things we are seeking to do cannot be done in our own strength. Prayer boasts in weakness, in order to more fully know God's strength. It is a "declaration of dependence," of need, of our weakness and God's strength. It is the cry of the weaker calling on the greater, in faith and belief that he can—and will—do something about it. In other words, prayer enacts the basic message of Christianity, the gospel itself. It's not the way we merit God's favor, but it's the way we receive it. Faith, expressed in prayer, is the empty hands that bring nothing but a willingness to receive the bread of life. Open, ready, and desperate to receive.

Prayer is what moves the kingdom forward. Prayer can move mountains; it can certainly shake our campuses. If we want the kingdom of God to come to our campus, we must pray. So how do we pray? Good thing Jesus taught us. In response to his disciples' request, "Lord, teach us to pray," Jesus answers with what we have come to know as the Lord's Prayer.

Pray like This

> Our Father in heaven,
> hallowed be your name,
> your kingdom come,
> your will be done,
> on earth as it is in heaven.
> Give us today our daily bread.
> And forgive us our debts,
> as we also have forgiven our debtors.
> And lead us not into temptation,
> but deliver us from the evil one. (Matthew 6:9-13)

Why did Jesus teach us to pray like this? In the context of Matthew 6, it seems he was concerned with two things in particular: people were using prayer "to be seen by men." In other words, their prayers weren't to God at all. They were just trying to look good. Praying for any other purpose than to commune with God is hypocrisy, according to Jesus.

The other thing Jesus says is: "Do not keep on babbling like pagans, for they think they will be heard because of their many words" (Matthew 6:7). It seems that some pagan pray-ers were overly talkative. As if God will pay more attention to us if we use more words. Hang around in Christian circles long enough and you know this isn't just a pagan problem. I've heard plenty of folks who sounded like they were only praying so the other people in the room would hear how holy they were. They used lots of words, especially big words. Sometimes they forced some emotion, or passion. That's not what Jesus is going for.

Many of us have come to know the Lord's Prayer as a sort of formula or magical incantation that we mindlessly recite. But if that's all we do with it, we've missed the point. Jesus intended it to be a starting point for our prayers. It shows us what we should be praying for and their relative importance to each other. With great economy of words, Jesus teaches us how to pray. This prayer is so familiar, even to people who aren't Christians, that we need to approach it with fresh ears. Here are a few things to note about the Lord's Prayer as a whole:[2]

Jesus' prayer is comprehensive. These petitions are incredibly direct and concise, but they pack an awful lot of meaning. Everything we could possibly need to pray about is included under the headings of these different petitions. Nothing is left out. This is the most comprehensive prayer we could ever pray, if we consider it as an instructive outline.

This helps us find a healthy balance in our prayers and gives us a guide so that we have ideas of what to pray for. All the petitions should be prayed; none should be neglected. Once you get going, you might find that the petition, "your kingdom come," is where you may spend most of your time in prayer.

The Lord's Prayer can be broken down into seven petitions.

1. **Our Father in heaven**. We start off with God, because it's about him, not us. He's the focus. And yet, we can call him Father. We can approach him. This petition reminds us of the scandal of the gospel, that we can approach the King of the Universe as his children.

2. **Hallowed be your name**. This tells us how to approach God. To "hallow" something is to make something holy, to set it apart as special, sacred, and of greatest importance. In other words, to worship. Right after we address our Father, we worship his name.

3. **Your kingdom come**. Now we ask God to bring his rule and his peace into the world around us. We welcome him into this very specific time and place we are inhabiting on earth.

4. **Your will be done, on earth as it is in heaven**. This is closely related to the kingdom petition. Both petitions cause us to ask what things could look like in their renewed and redeemed state.

5. **Give us today our daily bread**. See Proverbs 30:8-9. When we relationally depend on the Father, we grow in love and faithfulness. Jesus knew this. He was saying, in essence, "Don't give me so much that I think I can make it on my own, but neither give me so little that I become desperate." Christ knew what it meant to ask God for a daily portion.

6. **Forgive us our debts, as we also have forgiven our debtors**. Kingdom people are forgiven people who quickly forgive others. We don't hold grudges, keep records, or seek revenge. The only score we keep is what God has done for us in Christ. Because we know how much our Father has loved us, we love others radically and generously—especially if they don't deserve it.

7. **And lead us not into temptation, but deliver us from the evil one**. There's a spiritual battle going on. We are combatants in it, and if we are unaware, we are at risk of being taken out. "Be alert and of sober mind. Your enemy the devil prowls around like a roaring lion looking for someone to devour" (1 Peter 5:8).

We should notice that the prayer builds on itself; the order matters. For instance, it is good that "your kingdom come" is before the petition for our own needs, or "daily bread." I don't know about you, but when I think about the order and relative importance of the Lord's Prayer, I'm ashamed at how quickly I jump to the daily bread category. Our needs are important enough to pray for, but we have priorities here, and God's kingdom comes before our needs.

Prayer is the breath we need to live. Life comes from God; so communication with him is vital. Prayer ought to be so much more than a heavenly grocery list. It should move us. Prayers in which we are unmoved won't be very moving to God either, because they fail to communicate with God as a person. Think about conversations you have with loved ones: Do you spend the whole time telling them, "This is what I'd like to get from you"? Of course not—you pour out your heart, both the momentous and the trivial. You praise them, tell them what you love about them. Sometimes, you skip the talking and just seek to spend time with them. Should it be any different with God? And yet, how often do we simply say a "Dear God," rattle off our list, and punctuate it with an "Amen"? It's not that God doesn't hear such prayers; he does. But look how clearly we've just shown God that we have no desire to commune with him. No wonder it feels like our prayers are these weak, flabby things that barely get off the ground.

Use Your Holy Imagination!

When we pray, "your kingdom come, your will be done, on earth as it is in heaven," our holy imaginations should be sparked. In Matthew, the kingdom is called the "kingdom of heaven." We're praying that heaven's reality would break through into this world. What would it look like for God's *shalom* to rest on us? What would it look like for reconciliation to replace alienation? What would it look like for people, relationships, and even institutions to be made whole and flourish? How could we better reflect our Creator?

I find that stretching our holy imaginations is helpful in praying, "Your kingdom come." A good exercise for your friends or small group is to brainstorm what it would look like to see Jesus reign on your campus. What would be different? What would be better? What would no longer happen? Spend some time imagining things like this:

- What if your school was known more for what God was doing than for the success of the sports teams or its *US News* rankings?
- What if more people went to church on Sunday than to football on Saturday afternoon or to the clubs and parties on Friday night?
- What if people treated each other not as objects but as people created in God's image? What if there were no rape, sexual assault, or physical violence on your campus? What if there was no physical, emotional, or sexual abuse?
- What if people who hated each other were reconciled and loved each other?
- What if there were no crime and no need for campus police? What if no one stole bikes, objects from dorm rooms, or even things from the Internet?
- What if people loved what they were learning instead of feeling bored and restless? What if they didn't view education merely as a way to get a job later on (or a way to get wealthy) but a way to understand the world God has made?
- What if there were no outcasts but instead everyone was welcomed, loved, and accepted?
- What if people weren't alienated from themselves and didn't suffer from mental illness? What if there were no meds, no counselors, and no clinics? What if people lived in contented humility, not needing to puff themselves up or tear others down? What if people didn't hate themselves?
- What would fraternities and sororities look like if they truly existed to build up the concepts of brotherhood and sisterhood?

- What if people didn't agonize over their existence or their purpose in life? What if they trusted God to lead the way?

All of these things—and much more—are kingdom things, and they are the types of things we can and should be praying for.

Do these results sound far-fetched? Consider the Welsh Revival of 1904-5. Estimates are that over 150,000 people were converted during the first six months of the revival, and there were sweeping effects on the country. Numerous reports indicated that the bars were empty. People who used to waste their money getting drunk gave it to the church and the poor. Crime became so rare that it was common for judges to show up to work only to find no cases waiting for them. People put in a better day's work, paid back their debts, and reconciled with their enemies. It happened on a huge scale, and it happened as a result of prayer.

Are we praying this way? Both privately and with others? Do we believe that we are powerless apart from God, that apart from him we can do nothing, but that with God all things are possible?

Pray for the Kingdom to Come in Your Own Heart

The kingdom is advancing and taking over new territory. This includes your heart. We should be praying for God's kingdom to take over the unconquered areas of our hearts. One of the most common signs of a self-kingdom is anxiety. Anxiety shows us what we're not trusting God for. Jesus tells us not to worry in Matthew 6, because worry is a lack of trust. Worry is a sin against our all-sufficient, all-powerful, all-loving, all-providing God. No wonder Paul commands us, "Do not be anxious about anything, but in every situation, by prayer and petition, with thanksgiving, present your requests to God" (Philippians 4:6). In other words, don't worry or be anxious—pray. You're going to spend time thinking about things one way or another—better to pray about it than to simply dwell on it in your mind.

While prayer declares us dependent on God, worry is a sign we see ourselves independent of God. Anxiety is a symptom of dethroning God in our lives, of living as if we're godlike in a certain area. Anxiety is the fruit of believing "I can do it. I can handle it. I can manage things myself"—and then realizing we can't. Worrying and trying to fix it ourselves feels more immediate—at least we're doing something. But ironically, our attempts to be in control (to be God) make us more anxious, not less.

Prayer allows us to re-enthrone God at the center of our hearts. In prayer, I am humbled and reminded of how dependent I am, but I am also comforted that I have a God who cares for me. Peter writes, "Cast all your anxiety on him because he cares for you" (1 Peter 5:7). Here's how we do that in prayer.

1. **Draw near to God.** Spend time with God in his Word. You can't reach him with your anxieties if you're far away. As Pastor Darrin Patrick says, "The reason you don't trust God with your future is because you're not experiencing him in your present." This is why Jesus can say, "Do not worry . . . your heavenly Father knows [what] you need" (Matthew 6:31-32). If we are near him, we will know his heart for us.

2. **Name and identify your fears and anxieties.** Get specific. Pour them out in detail to God. Other people will tune you out, but he never tires or sleeps (Psalm 121:4).

3. **Confess, with humility, your inability** to handle, manage, defeat, conquer, or overcome these things.

4. **Confess, with humble joy, Christ's sufficiency.** Jesus and his death and resurrection are more than sufficient for all that you face. If God has proven faithful to you in your greatest need, how much more can we trust him with these little things?

5. **Cast it! Fling it!** Lay it down. Surrender. Tell God that you are giving this to him. Pray something like, "Father, I can't carry this load, but you can. So I cast it on you. You'll have to take it from here."

6. **Repeat.** Keep doing it. This casting is not a one-time project but ongoing. The bigger or harder your source of anxiety, the more frequently you'll have to give it over to him. Daily, sometimes hourly. Repeat as often as needed.

The Struggle of Prayer

Is prayer hard for you? Good. Join the club. It's not supposed to be easy. It's a struggle. Paul said his friend Epaphras agonized in prayer for the Colossian church (Colossians 4:12; some Bible translations say he "wrestled" or "struggled"). Prayer is not escape from the problems of the world but an engagement with them, crying out to the one who has the power to do something about them. It's a battle. As John Piper said, prayer is the walkie-talkie on the battle lines of spiritual warfare.[3] The faith-filled Christian isn't passive or fatalistic because "God will just take care of it." Rather, he or she is deeply engaged in prayer, struggling and wrestling with all his or her might. Why does prayer often feel like a struggle?

Prayer in which we never break a sweat, never shed a tear, never move to a posture of dependence and supplication on our knees—who is to know if we mean it? We may not even know ourselves. Do your prayers go unanswered? Well, have you ever been moved to your knees, broken a sweat, cried out till you were hoarse? Or are you more occupied with what you'll have for dinner or watch on TV tonight than this supposedly great matter you want to pray over? I don't mean you don't care about it, but you have never wrestled with God over it. God may withhold the answer until we know for ourselves that we have earnestly sought him and are utterly dependent on him. Do you take God at his word—that faith can move mountains? Prayer springs from, asks for, and leads to that kind of faith.

Many of us, I'm afraid, never get to this point. Brennan Manning calls what we suffer with "the agnosticism of inattention,"[4] or I would say the agnosticism of distraction. Many things cause this: lack of personal discipline, media saturation, sensory overload, shallow reading, sterile conversation, and perfunctory prayers. Our awareness of the present, risen, and active Christ can grow dim. When we pray, we must believe he exists (Hebrews 11:6).

Sometimes God may not answer our prayers right away, in order to prove our earnestness. It may also be God's way of breaking down the barriers between us and him. Our secret, defeating sins are uncovered and lay bare before him. Our deepest questions, our deepest wounds, our false assumptions, our most explosive accusations—all these are exposed before God in prayer.

We see this in the famous story of Jacob wrestling with God in Genesis 32. Jacob thought his biggest problem was all the people who were chasing him and trying to get revenge. But God met him in the middle of the night to show Jacob that his biggest problem wasn't with all those people—it was first and foremost with God. God is about to pour out a blessing on Jacob and to fundamentally change him, but before he builds him up he has to first break him down.

The story tells us that Jacob and the angel wrestled all night. Why did it go that long? Couldn't the angel have easily tossed Jacob into the atmosphere? Yes. The angel wrestled him all night in order to wear Jacob out, to exhaust him, so that he would finally come to the end of himself and make that admission of defeat that was also a confession of faith: "I will not let go unless you bless me" (v 26). Only when Jacob's strength was gone did the blessing come, did he get the name Israel, signifying the blessing of the nation that would come from him. Did you know that Jacob's new name, "Israel," means "one who struggles with

God, and prevails"? As we wrestle with God, and allow him to work his purpose in us, we will come to know the victory only he can give.

Jacob was renamed Israel, but there was another episode where the true Israel, Jesus himself, the perfect representative of all God's people, wrestled in prayer through the night on our behalf, struggling for our redemption. He stared the weight of humanity's sin in the face, and the cost of atoning for it, and this was so weighty that the Gospels say he was "deeply disturbed and troubled . . . overwhelmed with sorrow to the point of death" (Mark 14:33-34; Matthew 26:37-38).

If anyone's prayer life should have come easily, it would be Jesus', right? Not so: "During the days of Jesus' life on earth, he offered up prayers and petitions with fervent cries and tears to the one who could save him from death, and he was heard because of his reverent submission" (Hebrews 5:7). How much more should our prayer lives be full of passion and energy, even agony?

So suit up and get down to it. One word of encouragement, though: If you, like the disciples, tend to fall asleep when it's time to pray, remember that Jesus wrestled in prayer for his disciples who couldn't stay awake, then he went to the cross for them and us. And now, he's risen, and praying for us still.

Biblical Prayers

As we use our holy imaginations to pray for kingdom breakthroughs, we should pray God's words back to him.

Pray the Great Prayers

In addition to the Lord's Prayer, we have many other prayers included in the Bible, like Daniel's intercessory prayer in Daniel 9; Paul's prayer in Ephesians 3:14-21; Nehemiah's prayer in Nehemiah 1; Jesus' high-priestly prayer in John 17; the believer's prayer in Acts 4:23-31; and many more. Use them as models and guides to shape your prayers.

Pray the Great Commandments

Pray the Ten Commandments from Exodus 20; pray also Jesus' summary of them in Matthew 22:37-40: "'Love the Lord your God with all your heart and with all your soul and with all your mind.' This is the first and greatest commandment. And the second is like it: 'Love your neighbor as yourself.' All the Law and the Prophets hang on these two commandments."

Pray for the Great Commission to be fulfilled (Matthew 28:16-20), and pray the more than fifty "one another" commands found in the Bible.

Pray the Great Promises

God has not asked us to do anything that he has not also supplied the means for. He has given us great promises, so that we will pray with faith and confidence. Some of my favorites include:

Call to me and I will answer you and tell you great and unsearchable things you do not know. (Jeremiah 33:3)

Ask and it will be given to you; seek and you will find; knock and the door will be opened to you. (Luke 11:9)

His divine power has given us everything we need for a godly life through our knowledge of him. (2 Peter 1:3)

If anyone is in Christ, the new creation has come. The old has gone, the new is here! (2 Corinthians 5:17)

And my God will meet all your needs according to the riches of his glory in Christ Jesus. (Philippians 4:19)

And God is able to bless you abundantly, so that in all things at all times, having all that you need, you will abound in every good work. (2 Corinthians 9:8)

The LORD himself goes before you and will be with you; he will never leave you nor forsake you. Do not be afraid; do not be discouraged. (Deuteronomy 31:8)

If you remain in me and my words remain in you, ask whatever you wish, and it will be done for you. (John 15:7)

You did not choose me, but I chose you and appointed you so that you might go and bear fruit—fruit that will last—and so that whatever you ask in my name the Father will give you. (John 15:16)

And surely I am with you always, to the very end of the age. (Matthew 28:20)

Being confident of this, that he who began a good work in you will carry it on to completion until the day of Christ Jesus. (Philippians 1:6)

These promises begin to form the backbone of our prayers, because we know God must be true to himself and that therefore these promises will come true or are coming true right now.

One final word: don't fall prey to the common prayer-killers. Shallow and superfluous prayer requests have killed many a prayer meeting. I'm not saying that praying for your friend's sore throat is bad, but in the grand scheme of things, such things may not matter as much as some of the other kingdom things we could be praying for. Also, avoid the tendency to hold self-focused prayer sessions, where 90 percent of the sharing is about the people in the prayer circle. Prayer should broaden our perspective to the larger world. Finally, avoid the tendency to do more talking than actual praying. There's nothing worse than a "prayer meeting" that doesn't get around to actual prayer. Speaking of which, enough talking—let's get praying.

CHAPTER 6

SCRIPTURE STUDY: Matthew 6:5-15, and the many verses on prayer found in this chapter.

Discussion Questions

1. How's your prayer life? How often do you pray, and what do you pray about?

2. What about prayer comes easily to you? What is difficult?

3. In the chapter, we read about some of the promises of God answering prayer. Which of these promises was most helpful to you?

4. God has good reasons for working through prayer. Not only is he glorified, but we are changed when we pray. Review pages 68-69. What ways does prayer work on us?

5. How should the order of the Lord's Prayer be a reflection of our priorities?

6. How can you stretch your holy imagination in prayer? Spend some time brainstorming and praying some of the "what if" questions on pages 72-73.

SEVEN PROVOCATIVE FAITH

A few years ago, I discipled a student named Tyler who has a huge heart for reaching Muslim students with the gospel. He began to learn about their beliefs and culture. He went to some of their Muslim Student Association meetings and began befriending some of the students. He stuck out, because he was obviously the only non-Muslim there.

After one meeting, the president of the organization, the son of an Imam, asked Tyler to grab a meal with him. Tyler was thrilled. He anticipated some small talk at first, but the first question out of Shahid's mouth as they sat down was, "What's your problem with the Koran?" Whoa! Tyler was taken aback. How do you respond to a question like that?

For many of us, this scenario would be intimidating. Would you know how to respond? Could you respond in a way that would leave room for friendship? Tyler could. In a lot of ways, this was the response he had been hoping, praying, and preparing for. He wanted to talk about meaningful issues. He just hadn't expected to get there so quickly.

Tyler could respond because he was prepared. He was taking Arabic. He had studied the Koran. He'd studied the issues from a Christian perspective. He had been learning about Muslims in the context of relationships, and he counted many Muslims among his friends. He had even had conversations like this before. So when confronted with such a bold question, he could graciously, tactfully, and winsomely respond. That conversation led to many others where Tyler was able to share the gospel. To this day, Tyler reaches out to Muslims with the good news.

You may not know much about the Koran, or have Muslim students asking you about it. But the point is this: Tyler's presence provoked a response, and when it did, he was prepared.

Does our faith provoke a response from others? And are we ready when it does?

Who Made You King of Anything?

Responding to a direct question is only one of our challenges. There's also the widespread opinion, well expressed in Sara Bareilles' song "King of Anything." In the chorus, she communicates what a lot of people think about Christians who share their faith.

> *I hate to break it to you, babe*
> *But I'm not drowning*
> *There's no one here to save*
>
> *Who cares if you disagree?*
> *You are not me*
> *Who made you king of anything?*
> *So you dare tell me who to be*
> *Who died and made you king of anything?*[1]

How do we share our faith when it is so unwelcome, when even the idea of telling someone that they are drowning apart from Jesus is offensive?

The modern Christian is in quite a dilemma. On one side we have Muslims, atheists, and others who are utterly convinced of their beliefs and want to argue with us about it. There are a lot of reasons-to-believe to keep straight in our heads. On the other side, we have people with the "King of Anything" mentality, who are happy to let us believe what we want as long as it doesn't interfere with their beliefs.

To handle these situations in fruitful, effective ways, we need more than well-reasoned arguments and techniques. We need a provocative faith.

Everyone Who Asks

Peter's first letter is one of the most helpful places in the Bible to find directions on how to have a provocative faith in a non-Christian world. Peter writes to Christians who are a misunderstood, disliked, and sometimes even persecuted minority, which we can increasingly identify with in the post-Christian West.

Finally, all of you, be like-minded, be sympathetic, love one another, be compassionate and humble. Do not repay evil with evil or insult with insult. On the contrary, repay evil with blessing, because to this you were called so that you may inherit a blessing. For, "Whoever would love life and see good days must keep their tongue from evil and their lips from deceitful speech. They must turn from evil and do good; they must seek peace and pursue it. For the eyes of the Lord are on the righteous and his ears are attentive to their prayer, but the face of the Lord is against those who do evil."

Who is going to harm you if you are eager to do good? But even if you should suffer for what is right, you are blessed. "Do not fear their threats; do not be frightened." But in your hearts revere Christ as Lord. Always be prepared to give an answer to everyone who asks you to give the reason for the hope that you have. But do this with gentleness and respect, keeping a clear conscience, so that those who speak maliciously against your good behavior in Christ may be ashamed of their slander. For it is better, if it is God's will, to suffer for doing good than for doing evil. For Christ also suffered once for sins, the righteous for the unrighteous, to bring you to God. He was put to death in the body but made alive in the Spirit. (1 Peter 3:8-18)

This passage has so much to tell us on how to live faithfully in a world that doesn't accept Christians or our faith. But I'm particularly struck by Peter's instruction in verse 15: "Give an answer to *everyone who asks you* to give the reason for the hope that you have" (emphasis added). Did you catch that? Peter assumes people will be asking. It's a given that they'll ask.

In other words, people look at Christians, and say, "I noticed that even when people were making fun of you, you didn't get angry or make fun of them in return. How did you do that?" Or, "Everyone is so stressed out right now, and you have this peace. How can you be like that?" Or, "You and your friends really seem to care about each other, even love each other. My friends aren't like that. How did you get those kinds of friends?" This is what I mean by provocative faith. It stands out. It begs the question. It compels a response. It is not easily understood or categorized. It cannot be put in a box. Do you have a faith that provokes questions?

When we look in the New Testament, we see provocative faith on display. The early Christians were bold in preaching and teaching the faith. They were fearless in sharing all their possessions and in their willingness to suffer for their faith. The combination of their words and deeds, empowered by the Holy Spirit, could not be ignored. It forced people to think. It challenged, surprised, and transformed individuals, towns, and eventually the known world. It was nothing if not provocative.

I use the word "provocative" intentionally. Provocative means to "call forth" a response. To arouse a feeling or action, to incite, to stir up purposely, to provide the needed stimulus for discussion. For our purposes, we will say that *provocative Christianity is a faith—in word and deed—that calls forth a response.*

The gospel provokes a response. If it's at work in us, our words and deeds should be compelling people to ask us about the hope that we have. When was the last time your words and deeds forced someone to ask you about your beliefs or lifestyle? If our faith never compels anyone to respond—whether positively or negatively—we're doing it wrong.

Reasons We Don't Give the Reason

My fear is that for many of us, our day-to-day faith does not provoke anything except yawns. The boldness and fearlessness that characterized the early believers, or more modern-day "saints," seem pretty foreign to us. But before we get to what it means to have a provocative faith, we need to look at some of the obstacles we face.

We often think, "I don't know what to say." For some of us, the thought of ending up in a conversation like Tyler's is enough to induce a panic attack. Perhaps you feel out of your depth when conversations with classmates or coworkers take a serious turn. Or you don't know how to lead the conversation toward substantial faith issues, even when you want to. Have you ever found yourself with unbelieving coworkers during downtime at work, and the jokes, stories, language, tone, and content of the conversation is objectionable? You don't want to curse, complain, laugh at dirty jokes, and so forth—and so you sit, uncomfortably silent, in the corner. With nothing good to say, you say nothing at all. Or you feel like you've been labeled (as an "evangelical" or "fundamentalist" or "born again"), and put in a box, so people don't really listen to you, even when you do speak up.

Or we think, "I'm afraid of how people will respond." Do you ever fear what people might think or say if you really do share your faith clearly? Do you have categories in your head of people you could or couldn't share with? Think back on the religious conversations you've had. Have you ever felt reactive, scrambling to cover the bases, defensive, just trying to make Christianity look respectable without messing up? Ever felt your confidence shaken—if not in your faith, at least in your ability to express it?

Or perhaps we don't speak up because we think, "I'm embarrassed by the extreme and uncharitable stances other Christians take." Christians usually get lumped together, which isn't accurate or fair. But how will people know any different unless we tell them? It's on us to dispel the stereotypes and change the perceptions. That doesn't mean we'll make everyone happy, but it's our responsibility to do our part to change the conversation.

If any of these reasons apply to you, you're not alone. Many Christians out there feel like this. A recent study showed that 61 percent of regular church attenders "have not told another person about how to become a Christian in the previous six months."[2] We don't know how to get out of the box society has put us in. We don't know how to get around all the assumptions and biases. We feel like "I'll never be smart enough, or brave enough, to share my faith." Fortunately, we don't have to stay there.

We have the best news to share. We are heralds and ambassadors—mouthpieces—of the good news, the gospel (2 Corinthians 5:11-21). We have the message that people need to hear. We need to be talking. We should have plenty to say. We cannot be silent.

The Source of Provocative Faith

We should have plenty to say, and yet we don't. What creates a provocative faith in us? Think back for a moment to the people who have had the greatest impact on your own faith. People like parents, teachers, friends, pastors, youth pastors, and campus ministers. My educated guess is that the people who have provoked the most faith in you have at least one trait in common: they give evidence of having been with Jesus. They talk like him. They listen like him. They serve like him. They love like him. You know they have been with him. And their faith called forth something in you and in many others.

This is what we see happening in the New Testament. In Acts 4, Peter and John are leading the explosion of the church. Thousands are being saved, the poor are being cared for, incredible prayers are being answered, and they're healing people right and left. They're also dealing with the first wave of persecution. All this activity provokes a response from the religious authorities, and Peter and John are dragged before them. Peter, "filled with the Holy Spirit" (v. 8), preaches one of his "let's just cut to the chase here" sermons. Here's his sermon outline:

1. Yes, amazing things are happening.

2. It's because of Jesus, whose death you're responsible for, but God raised him from the dead. So,

3. Jesus is the only way of salvation, and you need to be saved.

You can tell the religious leaders are a bit flummoxed here. "Who are these guys to talk to us like this?" Then—and I love this part—it says, "When they saw the courage of Peter and John and realized that they were unschooled, ordinary men, they were astonished and *they took note that these men had been with Jesus*" (Acts 4:13, emphasis added).

Provocative faith is the result of being with Jesus. This means that all the evangelistic techniques and tools in the world won't accomplish much of anything if we haven't been with him. Revere Christ by putting him first. Commit to spending time with him. Get to know his Word. Pray regularly. Commit to Jesus' body, the church. Do whatever you have to do to be with Jesus. Then, and only then, will we have a provocative faith, a faith that is worth sharing with others.

Ten Ways to Live Out Provocative Faith like Jesus

Once we've tapped into the source of provocative faith by committing to being with Jesus, we need to ask what it looks like to live out this faith. We dishonor the King we represent when we are ashamed, fearful, embarrassed, or defensive. We need to look no further than Jesus to see how he communicated his message. He was relentlessly provocative. Our character and our methods should be Christlike. When doubts arise, remember what Jesus told his disciples: "Peace be with you! As the Father has sent me, I am sending you" (John 20:21).

Throughout the Gospels, he's calling forth a response. So should we. Here are ten ways we can provoke like Jesus.

1. Provocative Faith Is Urgent

Jesus doesn't waste any time. His interactions with others are intentional and to the point. When he spies little Zacchaeus up in the sycamore tree, he says, "Zacchaeus, hurry and come down, for I must stay at your house today" (Luke 19:5, ESV). The gospel writers, especially Mark, are constantly talking about how Jesus "immediately" said this or did that, and how people's response was also immediate. To be around Jesus was to see a holy sense of urgency at work. That didn't mean Jesus was a busybody or never stopped moving. On the contrary, he felt a deep sense of urgency to pray and be with his Father, sometimes all night. But no matter what he was doing, Jesus looked to make the most of every encounter and situation.

2. Provocative Faith Asks, "Why?" (and Lots of Other Good Questions)

Read the Gospels and you notice how often Jesus refuses to answer the question that he's asked. He usually responds with a question of his own—the question they should be asking or what he wants to talk about. Many times, he'll simply ask open-ended questions, especially: "Why do you ask me that?"

In having faith conversations with dozens of unbelievers, I've found that often the most helpful and provocative question is simply "Why?" This isn't just a spiritual deflection tactic. This is a question designed to get at someone's real question. In my experience, people rarely come out with the questions closest to their hearts. Instead, their questions are their own attempts at deflection, as they throw up objections to the gospel based on evolution, sexuality, other religions, politics, church history, and more. These can and should be answered but with the greater goal of helping people see who Jesus is. Get to the real question.

3. Provocative Faith Is Offensive

It seems all too easy to offend people these days, even when we're trying not to. I understand the desire to not be confused with Westboro Baptist or some other fundamental types. However, the reality is that the gospel, faithfully communicated, will be offensive to some people. Paul talks about "the offense of the cross" in Galatians 5:11 (see also Romans 9:33 and 1 Peter 2:8). Some people are offended that Jesus is the only way to salvation (the gospel is too narrow). Others are offended that God will forgive anyone who puts faith in Jesus, even a serial killer (the gospel is too broad). Others are offended that the Bible forbids certain behaviors that they approve of (for example, sexual immorality).

The gospel says that we are sinners, powerless to save ourselves, and that we need a Savior. Those who truly hear that will feel a hit to their pride. At some level, we all want to believe we can save ourselves or that we don't need Jesus. Regardless, we have to expect that at some point people will be offended. And we can't let that stop us. What is more important? Someone's momentary feelings or their eternal future? Saying, "I don't want to offend anyone," doesn't show that we care about them; rather, it shows that we don't care *enough*. This isn't to say that we have permission to go around offending people constantly. Let's be completely sure that it is the message of Jesus that is doing the offending, not something about us.

4. Provocative Faith Is Creative (and Tells Good Stories)

One reason I'm not a fan of "canned" gospel presentations (e.g., something based on a script or pamphlet) is that it can undermine our message. I view those tools as crutches. If you're limping along, you should use it. But you don't want to stay on crutches longer than you have to. If you always need a script, your message probably isn't coming from your heart. And it probably won't connect with your listener, unless he or she is really into scripts or pamphlets.

When we read the Gospels, we see how relentlessly creative Jesus was. He had to be. Think about how he must have felt, dwelling with the Father in all the glory of heaven, from all eternity, and then coming down here to dwell with humans. How could he possibly explain the glory of the kingdom of heaven? Don't you think he felt that his palette was a little limited? We humans have only five senses, three dimensions, and underused brains. So Jesus was creative and looked for ways to explain things to us in new and fresh ways, in ways that we would understand. This means some stories or illustrations we wouldn't expect.

5. Provocative Faith Throws a Good Party

Christians need to repent of throwing bad parties. I once had a student tell me, "I quit going to another ministry, because they had us building Popsicle stick structures. It was Friday night. I'm in college. I'm not playing with Popsicle sticks!" True that. Let's repent of believing that it's impossible to have fun without alcohol being the main ingredient. Jesus shows you don't have to sin to have fun. Throwing a good party is one way to use our creative gifts to speak and incarnate the gospel in fresh ways.

6. Provocative Faith Speaks

You may have heard the line attributed to Francis of Assisi, "Preach the Gospel at all times. If necessary, use words." You may have also heard how he never said that line, nor would he have. It's not accurate historically, and it's not accurate theologically. The gospel is a message. It must be spoken. It has content—it can't be absorbed by osmosis. Paul makes this clear in Romans.

"The word is near you, in your mouth and in your heart" (that is, the word of faith that we proclaim); because, if you confess with your mouth that Jesus is Lord and believe in your heart that God raised him from the dead, you will be saved. For with the heart one believes and is justified, and with the mouth one confesses and is saved. For the Scripture says, "Everyone who believes in him will not be put to shame." For there is no distinction between Jew and Greek; for the same Lord is Lord of all, bestowing his riches on all who call on him. For "everyone who calls on the name of the Lord will be saved."

But how are they to call on him in whom they have not believed? And how are they to believe in him of whom they have never heard? And how are they to hear without someone preaching? And how are they to preach unless they are sent? As it is written, "How beautiful are the feet of those who preach the good news!" (Romans 10:8-15, ESV)

How indeed! I'm all for preaching the gospel with our actions (see the next point), but our actions cooperate with our words. Jesus is our model here. He did incredible things and led a perfect, sinless life. He was the Word in presence, deed, and speech. He wasn't simply a metaphorical word, a silent doer: He spoke. He taught. He preached. If Jesus' actions alone weren't sufficient to communicate the gospel, how much more should we be sharing the message. At some point, you have to open your mouth. Actions alone won't cut it.

7. Provocative Faith Serves

At the same time, words alone are also insufficient. In our cultural situation, words are cheap. They must be backed up by lives of integrity and service—as God designed for them to be. Here again, Jesus is our example. "Whoever wants to become great among you must be your servant, and whoever wants to be first must be slave of all. For even the Son of Man did not come to be served, but to serve, and to give his life as a ransom for many" (Mark 10:43-45).

It's both our example and our words. It's our lives and our lips. Jesus came both speaking and serving. People often emphasize one at the expense of the other. Words without actions that back them up are empty. But actions unaccompanied by words can also be empty if they are unintelligible. When we serve others, we can surprise them with grace, meet practical needs, and demonstrate the love of God that is proclaimed in the gospel.

8. Provocative Faith Invites

When provocative faith takes root, something always happens. People get excited—so excited that they have to invite everyone else they know to check it out. The joy and power of what they've experienced spreads like wildfire through their relational networks. We see this with the woman at the well in John 4. After realizing who Jesus is, this former outcast goes back to the entire town that had rejected her and tells them to come hear the man who "'told me everything I ever did' . . . and because of [Jesus'] words many more became believers. They said to the woman, 'We no longer believe just because of what you said; now we have heard for ourselves, and we know that this man really is the Savior of the world'" (vv. 39, 41-42).

We also see this with the disciples when they encounter Jesus. Andrew goes and gets his brother, some guy named Cephas, telling him, "We have found the Messiah" (John 1:41). Then Philip gets his brother Nathaniel, "We have found the one Moses wrote about . . . come and see" (John 1:45-46). The invitation to "come and see" is part of provoking a response in others. In my experience, many students are afraid to do this. They don't think anyone will be interested. Or they give up after one halfhearted invitation. But the more provocative our faith is, the more others will be curious and ultimately drawn to Jesus. Don't hesitate to make that invitation.

9. Provocative Faith Is Always Ready to Give the Reason for the Hope

The phrase "give the reason," is *apo logos* in Greek. It's where we get the word "apologetics." Apologetics is often called "the defense of the faith," and it's a branch of theology concerned with explaining why we believe what we believe. Our faith is not irrational, and it's not blind. It is rational, it is reasonable, and it's a different way of seeing. We have good reasons to believe what we do. You should be able to not simply say what you believe but also why. You should be able to give as coherent an explanation of why you believe what you believe as possible. Can you do that?

But keep in mind what I said earlier about the importance of being with Jesus. A lot of very smart and educated Christian apologists have won the debate but missed the point. We need more than reasoned argumentation. This isn't just a head activity; it's a heart one as well. As you give the hope that you have, don't just talk about why the Bible is true because of the mountains of evidence we have (though we do). Share about how it sustains you, how it encourages you, how God's Word cuts to the heart and gets you out of bed in the morning. Share about how Christ gives you hope and joy and peace. This isn't just about arguing with skeptics; this is encouraging people who feel discouraged, depressed, hopeless, and defeated. And we have the privilege of offering them the certain hope of Christ.[3]

10. Provocative Faith Speaks with Gentleness and Respect

If your campus is like mine, you have some preachers who come and scream hellfire and damnation at passing students. They're usually pretty angry, and they are usually talking about sex, evolution, and rock and roll. You know the type. These guys actually present us with a golden opportunity to talk about the gospel, because they gather the crowd and start the conversation. Then we can come in and say, "I'm a Christian, but this is what I believe, and this is how I think it should be shared." I've started many a conversation with onlookers that way.

One of my most memorable moments in ministry came when a man—I believe his name was Shawn the Baptist, I kid you not—called me a "wolf" because I was sharing the gospel of grace with so many of his audience that he felt disrupted and threatened. But let me clarify something. The reason we don't rant and rave isn't because it's socially unacceptable. It's because harshness and disrespect in the sharing of the gospel is forbidden. In their "zeal" to spread the gospel, these traveling hellfire preachers disobey the Bible. Peter's words in 1 Peter 3:15 are some of the clearest instructions for how to share our faith—and it's not with unrighteous anger or mocking or force or violence. The gospel-telling is neither fight nor flight—it is faithful engagement.[4]

Ready for Your Divine Appointment?

Always be ready. You never know when people will want to know or ask to know. Have you ever had a divine appointment? That is, a meeting, encounter, or event that you didn't schedule but God undoubtedly did. I had one of those a couple of years ago when the president came to speak on campus.

The POTUS's appearance was a hot ticket, and I hadn't planned on waiting in line for hours to get one. But when my friend called me the night before with an extra ticket, I jumped at the chance.

I showed up the next morning with a few thousand other people and we waited in line for all the necessary security checks, then moved to the arena where we continued to wait for the president to arrive. All told, we had nearly three hours to burn off. I started chatting with the woman sitting next to me, mostly small talk. I could tell she was a foreign grad student, probably Chinese—not uncommon at our school. I looked over and saw she was reading a pamphlet of the Gospel of John. She was in the middle of John 3.

I said, "I see you're reading the Bible. What do you think of it?"

She replied, "It's interesting, but I have a lot of questions."

Now that my pastoral antennae were quivering, I said, "It's funny you should say that. I'm a minister. What are your questions?"

She smiled a little, then asked, "This is a story, right?"

"Yes, it's a story. I believe it's a true story."

"Does it dishonor the god if I read it as just a story?"

"Well, I think the story was written to get you to think, to get you to ask why so many people believe it's true."

From there, we talked about Jesus being both God and man, and I showed her some of his claims to divinity through the "I AM" statements in John.

At one point she asked, "So this says Jesus is God. What's the point?"

I responded with another question: "Imagine you were God. Would you do it this way? Would you reveal yourself and save the world this way? Why do you think God would do it this way?"

We talked about the significance of the cross and the difference between the gospel and religion. (Being from communist China, both the gospel and religion were foreign to her.) She was really tracking with our conversation, and at times stopped so she could think and ponder her next question.

Being packed in the stands, we were having this conversation in the hearing of several other people. I could tell some were listening as well. Before long, the president arrived, and our conversation came to an end. Afterward, Chelsea and I exchanged emails and said we'd meet again to continue our conversation. I discovered she knew a couple other Christians and had even visited my church a few times, as well as an international ministry at Penn State.

I walked away from that conversation and realized that while it was cool to hear the president in person, the highlight of my day had without a doubt been sharing the gospel with this student. I felt a bit like Philip after his encounter with the Ethiopian eunuch in Acts 8. Without my planning, I had been whisked away to share the gospel with someone already reading Scripture, asking, "What does this mean?"

Later I found out that my friend Brian had felt prompted by the Holy Spirit to offer me that ticket, thinking, "Maybe Steve will get to have a significant conversation with someone." My wife, Jess, also felt compelled to stop and pray for me that morning, without knowing why.

Chelsea and I met a few more times and had some good conversations, and then summer came and I lost track of her. Fast-forward two years later, and I found out that she had in fact become a Christian! I feel privileged that I got to play a small part in her coming to faith. And I believe I had a part to play because I was ready to have that conversation.

This kind of thing doesn't happen to me every day, but it was a reminder that God is always working, always setting up divine appointments. It was a reminder that there are people all around us who want to know what the gospel is. It's amazing how many more divine appointments we'll have when we're ready and willing to let our provocative faith show.

Are you ready for your divine appointment?

CHAPTER 7
SCRIPTURE STUDY: 1 Peter 3:8-22

Discussion Questions

1. How prepared are you to answer for your faith? Can you explain why you believe what you believe?

2. Is your faith proactive? When was the last time someone wanted to know why you believe what you believe? Does your faith compel people to ask?

3. Sharing the gospel with gentleness and respect should not result in a "fight or flight" instinct. Which side do you tend to fall on, and how can you move toward faithful engagement?

4. Which of the ten aspects of provocative faith is your strong suit? Which do you need to work on?

EIGHT EVERY SQUARE INCH

A while back, I spent a weekend with a group of students from Princeton University. They were part of Manna Christian Fellowship, a ministry group on campus. Joel Ristuccia and Sam Chez, two of their leaders, asked me to come and speak on the topic of "Redeeming Innovation: New Ideas for Making All Things New." I had a blast. Obviously, they were an intelligent group, but these students were fun, attentive, engaged, and welcoming. All weekend, we discussed ways they could join Jesus in "making all things new" (Revelation 21:5, ESV) on their campus. The weekend culminated with several small groups of students presenting their ideas of how they could transform their campus.

Among the ideas—many of which were excellent—was one to create an app for smartphones that would share prayer requests with a wide audience in real time, to encourage more people to pray for their friends and classmates. There were several ideas on how students could share their faith. But there were also some interesting ideas that weren't specifically about spiritual disciplines like prayer and evangelism. Several groups had ideas for how to get out of the "bubble" and serve their community. One group noted that social groups at Princeton were pretty closed and cliquish, especially at mealtimes, so they proposed some ways to change the entire social dynamic on campus, including changing who people ate with in the cafeterias and some ways to facilitate conversations that would form new relationships. Another group noted that students made unhealthy decisions around exam time, including doping themselves with way too much caffeine, so they proposed offering free health-food smoothies during finals. Last I checked, a few of these ideas were in production or had been tried successfully.

You might think, "That sounds cool and all . . . but why? Why should we care about social dynamics or fruit smoothies? If we're loving God and reading our Bibles, then who cares about all that other stuff? Besides, I'm busy enough as it is . . ." The answer is simple. We should care because God cares. Everything matters. Everything is spiritual. These are all kingdom issues. The Manna students understood that, and God is using them to bless their campus. The same can be true on your campus.

Everything Is Spiritual; Everything Matters

What would it look like for the kingdom to come, for God's *shalom* to reign, for your campus to flourish under Christ? Would it mean that everything would be the same, except more people go to church or your Christian group? Of course not. The list of things that would be different would be infinite. It would definitely include things like prayer and Bible reading. But it would also include the way people relate to one another, what they put into their bodies, and more. Everything is spiritual, not just what we narrowly label as spiritual.

We're developing a Christian worldview in this book—at least the beginnings of one—to help us faithfully engage our college worlds. There is a grand story of redemption that God is writing. But what does this mean for the everyday, nitty-gritty of college life? The answer is: everything. The grand story connects to our living, breathing, eating, drinking, working, studying, sporting, and playing lives.

Developing a Christian worldview includes far more than knowing your Bible. It's far more than having an answer to questions about abortion or homosexuality. It's far more than understanding all the "-isms" out there and how they match up against Christianity. A true and robust Christian worldview helps us see everything through the lens of the big story (the Christian metanarrative). If everything is my Father's world, that is, everything belongs to him, well then that changes everything.

This is my Father's world.

He shines in all that's fair.

In the rustling grass I hear him pass.

He speaks to me everywhere.[1]

Every Square Inch

"There is not a square inch in the whole domain of our human existence over which Christ, who is Sovereign over all, does not cry: 'Mine!'"[2] This is a bold statement. Every square inch, in all of creation, belongs to King Jesus. He claims it for himself, as his own. Jesus cries out "Mine!" with the same voice that thundered at Sinai and calmed the storm over Galilee. Every square inch rightfully belongs to him, as Creator, Redeemer, and King.

Abraham Kuyper understood this better than just about anyone. He lived his life as if his mission was to demonstrate Christ's kingship over every area of creation—personally. He was a modern-day Renaissance man/powerhouse, somehow fitting several highly accomplished careers into one lifetime. He was a pastor, theologian, media mogul, university founder and educator, and a politician—eventually becoming the prime minister of the Netherlands. He started two newspapers, founded a political party, helped start a new denomination, founded a university, and all the while preached, taught, and wrote. His influence on his country, and on many Christians today, is simply incredible. As prominent historian Mark Noll said about Kuyper, his career "was as filled with noteworthy achievement as that of any single individual in modern Western history."[3]

What's interesting about Kuyper is that he didn't start this way. A mediocre student in his early years, he latched on to theology and received his doctorate from the University of Leiden. But Leiden, at that time, was quite liberal theologically. It was one of those schools that studied theology but simultaneously doubted if Jesus was really raised from the dead, if the Bible was true, and more. Probably like some religion classes you've taken. Kuyper did well in this world, but it left him feeling empty and exhausted. On a vacation, he read *The Heir of Redclyffe*, a novel by Charlotte Yonge, whose main character showed him his own arrogance and spiritual emptiness. He was also won over by the simple yet profound faith of the people in his first church. This led him to leave behind his theologically liberal past and commit himself to the real, risen Christ; to the Bible as God's Word; to spiritual fervor combined with intellectual breadth and depth; and to reform in the church and the culture of the Netherlands. I tell you all this because when I share his ideas with you, you'll wonder if anyone could possibly do all of it. Kuyper did.

One of Kuyper's key contributions to a Christian worldview is the concept of "spheres." He taught that God has created the world with various cultural spheres, such as church, family, politics, business, art, education, and more.

These spheres are unique and distinct in what they do, working "each accord-ing to its kind" (Genesis 1:12, 21, 24; 7:14, ESV). They should interfere with each other as little as possible—what he called "sphere sovereignty." His thinking was that if Jesus is the King (or sovereign), then no other sphere should act as sovereign over another.

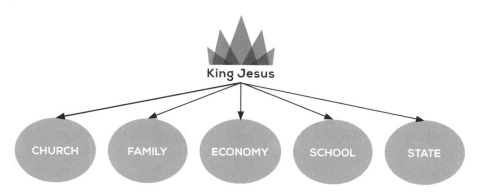

Let me demonstrate what this means for a debate that's common in our cul-ture today. The concept of spheres, in this sense, means that Kuyper is in favor of the (historic) separation of church and state. That is, that the church should not rule the state, and the state should not rule the church. Kuyper had observed that when spheres get confused, they don't do their jobs and their God-given work is corrupted. But Kuyper also argued—and this is key—that Christians have an obligation to be an influence for kingdom good in each of the cultural spheres. So Christians should faithfully engage the spheres of politics/govern-ment, education, art, and more. This runs directly against what many modern secularists think "separation of church and state" means today, which is that if you're a Christian you shouldn't "impose your beliefs" on others through the laws you make (if you're a lawmaker) or how you vote (if you're a citizen). As if non-Christians don't have worldviews and belief systems that guide them and direct how they live, worship, and vote.

Kuyper on Campus

Understanding cultural spheres has profound implications for how we ap-proach everyday life. The remainder of this book will flesh out what faithful engagement looks like in common campus spheres. The university is a sphere in itself, but it's unique in that it contains all the other spheres. I chose to focus

on five spheres of kingdom work on campus: church/Christian fellowship, relationships, academics/work, leadership, and the party scene.

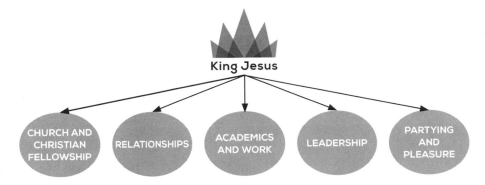

We might think of these spheres as the pillars of what hold the university
up, since pillars are common on so many campuses (and the inspiration for the
cover of this book). My list of five spheres is not exhaustive, by any means, but
those five pillars cover the primary functional spheres that we live in when we
hit the campus.

This way of thinking is incredibly helpful when it comes to our everyday,
living-and-breathing, eating-and-drinking lives. To see everything as belonging
to King Jesus, through these spheres, keeps us from shrinking him down. It
reminds us that all things will be reconciled to him (Colossians 1:20), that they
will be brought under his reign (Philippians 2:9-11), "so that in all things God
may be praised through Jesus Christ. To him be the glory and the power for ever
and ever. Amen" (1 Peter 4:11). This is a Christ-saturated, God-glorifying way
of viewing the world.

It also keeps us from putting God in a box and having a compartmentalized
faith. At first glance, it might seem that by partitioning off each sphere, compartmentalizing is exactly what we're doing. But it's actually the opposite. Each
sphere of life has a line that connects straight back to Christ, breaking down any
walls that keep him out. We're not putting God in a box—we're putting creation
in the boxes God designed for them. We're clearing the clutter, so that the King
has room to work.

Third, this worldview gives worth and dignity and purpose to all our work.
Everything we do matters. We worship God through all of it. As Peter says,
"You are a chosen people, a royal priesthood, a holy nation, God's special pos-
session, that you may declare the praises of him who called you out of darkness

into his wonderful light" (1 Peter 2:9). We function as a royal priesthood, offering up our very lives as pleasing offerings to God (Romans 12:1-2). Priests are individuals who speak to God for people, making offerings to God on behalf of the people. Christians are called to do that in every sphere of life, which is why we have all been commissioned for that task. Did you know that you are a priest for your campus? It's a big calling. Every sphere of college life is ripe, ready to be redeemed by and for the kingdom of God.

The Good, the Bad, and the Redeemed

Let's first seek out and affirm what is good about these spheres. Kuyper was a big proponent of the idea of "common grace," that some things are not irrevocably ruined but retain marks of God's goodness and are available to all. This means seeing God show up in some surprising places. We can look in a sphere like the arts and see truth portrayed in Shakespeare or a modern film and hear beauty in Mozart or contemporary music. Yes, there can be garbage and blasphemy mixed in too, but that does not negate the truth and beauty found alongside it. All the more reason why we need Christians to enter and participate in the art sphere. Not to make "religious" art but to create good art, good music, good films, and good literature.

> This is my Father's world,
>
> Dreaming, I see His face.
>
> I ope[n] my eyes, and in glad surprise
>
> Cry, "The Lord is in this place."[4]

Common grace is a reminder that "everything created by God is good, and nothing is to be rejected if it is received with thanksgiving, for it is made holy by the word of God and prayer" (1 Timothy 4:4-5, ESV). However, any talk of common grace must be tempered by the fact that everything has been broken by sin. You will recall that in the introduction we talked about the cross between two thieves—legalism and license. These two can manifest in our spheres. One thief would have us love a sphere far too little or rigidly; the other thief would have us love it far too much. One thief is about a misguided obedience that tries to earn our righteousness; the other is about a misguided freedom that abuses our forgiveness in Christ with cheap grace.

In the following chart you can see how the two thieves compete with the redeemed version of faithful living in each of the spheres.

SPHERE	THIEF 1 (LEGALISM)	THIEF 2 (LICENSE)	REDEEMED VIEW
Church	Church is exclusive	Church is optional	Church is an essential but not the exclusive place of God's working
Relationships	People-Judger: doesn't need or care for others	People-Pleaser: needs and cares too much	Love, serve, honor, and befriend people as created in the image of God
Academics	Overachiever: worships work and achievement	Slacker: worships fun; thinks work is a bad word	Work is a way to worship God; work hard, but not excessively
Leadership	Leadership means total control, the firmer the better	Leadership . . . Who needs it?	Serve, love, and influence with humility and courage
Party Scene	Fun is inherently evil; hide from it	"Ideahilism": fun means go crazy, life is short	True fun and pleasure are a gift from God that gives life and doesn't exploit

The Music of the Spheres

The remainder of this book will walk us through these spheres, so that we can better understand and experience faithfulness in every area of our lives. Our hope isn't just for ourselves though; it's that we would have a redemptive influence on those around us. Our hope is for our campuses—and ultimately the world—as well. What will it look like for the kingdom to come and for Christ's *shalom* to reign in every sphere of your life? How about on your campus? King Jesus is in the process of redeeming creation and reconciling all things to himself. We get to be part of that, one sphere at a time.

Let's find out what that looks like in the last third of the book, as we tackle church, relationships, academics, leadership, and the party scene.

> *This is my Father's world,*
>> *Should my heart be ever sad?*
> *The Lord is King—let the heavens ring.*
>> *God reigns—let the earth be glad.*
> *This is my Father's world.*
>> *Now closer to Heaven bound,*
> *For dear to God is the earth Christ trod.*
>> *No place but is holy ground.*[5]

CHAPTER 8

SCRIPTURE STUDY: Psalm 24

Discussion Questions

1. Do you tend to view your faith as just one sphere among many, or is Jesus over all spheres?

2. What will it look like for the kingdom to come and for Christ's *shalom* to reign in every sphere of your life? How about on your campus?

3. Where is it easiest to be a Christian on campus? Where is it hardest? Why?

4. Which of the five spheres mentioned are you most interested in discussing?

NINE CHURCH AND CHRISTIAN FELLOWSHIP

Let's begin with the church sphere (and, by extension, Christian fellowships). What I hope to make evident is that church is absolutely essential, but not the exclusive place of God's work. The church is not the same thing as the kingdom of God, but it is primarily through her that the kingdom comes. We can't say we're engaged in kingdom work if we're not connected to the church. We can't say we love the King if we don't love his bride. During the college years, it's crucial that you make a commitment to a local church and Christian fellowship, but also that you do not see it as the only place in which you're called to live faithfully.

You Need the Church, and the Church Needs You

Remember our talk of rest stops in the introduction? I see this very clearly when it comes to college students and church. The thought is that "I'm not here very long, I'm just passing through. I'm not going to do much more than attend (when it's convenient), so I'll hang back." So we end up with students acting like those people who fill the empty seats at the Academy Awards. They look good, but they're anonymous and ultimately irrelevant to what's going on. When it comes to church, are you just a seat-filler? Unfortunately, the seat-filler approach is a common mentality. But it's untrue and unhelpful. The truth is that the church needs students, and students need the church. What's most helpful for you, and the larger church, is to mutually involve and enfold each other in what you're doing. This is easier said than done, but it's worth pursuing. The church is a source of community that you cannot do without. For reasons I'll explain later, I don't believe your Christian fellowship group is the same thing. To be faithful to God's call, we need to pursue community in the places he's designed for it. There is nothing like the church when she is doing what God has designed for her to do. She is an unstoppable force. The three most common metaphors for the church in the New Testament are: building, bride, and body.

- Building—to display God's glory and manifest his presence (1 Peter 2)
- Bride—to display Christ's beauty and receive his love (Ephesians 5)
- Body—to do Christ's work and serve the world (1 Corinthians 12; Ephesians 4)

The building, bride, and body of Jesus Christ, the King of the Universe. This sounds like an exciting movement that I definitely want to participate in. But how does this connect to the ordinary expressions of church life, like small groups?

But What's the Point?

Christian community takes a lot of different shapes. If you're like many Christian college students, you are involved in some kind of small group: some food, some sharing and confession, some Bible study or book study and discussion, and some prayer.

Can I suggest that we need a reminder of *why* we pursue community? Why do we gather on Sunday mornings and Wednesday or Thursday nights? Why do we gather in church buildings, theaters and gyms, lounges and multipurpose spaces, dorm rooms and apartments? What's the point of community? Are there reasons that go beyond "because we've always done it that way"?

In his book *Community*, author Brad House writes,

I have heard many purposes for joining community groups, including but not limited to: belonging, making big church feel small, learning the Bible, pastoral care, fellowship, friends, closing the back door of the church, evangelism, and so on. . . . these "purposes" are in fact the product of community rather than its ultimate goal.[1]

If we don't regularly remind ourselves of the ultimate purpose, we will start to make the by-products the goal. Since many of those by-products are benefits to us, we'll decide to opt out if we're not getting what we think we should. We'll use some pious and sincere-sounding words, like "I'm just not being fed there," "It's too shallow for me," "I don't feel accepted; it's very cliquish," or something along those lines. I'm not saying those things aren't true, but I fear that we regularly prioritize our benefits over the larger purpose. When we do that, we miss the point. Here are a few key reasons why we need to pursue community in the church (this isn't exhaustive). Community is good for: Connection (the Building), Movement (the Bride), and Growth (the Body).

1. Connection (the Building)

We won't fully understand what we have in Jesus Christ if we are not connected to others. Peter puts it this way, "You also, like living stones, are being built into a spiritual house to be a holy priesthood, offering spiritual sacrifices acceptable to God through Jesus Christ" (1 Peter 2:5). In a building, the stones are right on top of each other. They're closely connected. And the more connected they are, the stronger and better the building will be.

This runs counter to the highly individualistic approach to spirituality (and everything else) that most of us default to in our society. But if you're not pursuing Jesus with other people, you won't experience Jesus in all his richness and depth.

I remember having this driven home as I studied one of my favorite verses in the Bible, tucked away in Paul's brief letter to Philemon.

"I pray that your partnership with us in the faith may be effective in deepening your understanding of every good thing we share for the sake of Christ" (Philemon 6).

In this verse Paul uses the Greek word *koinonia*, which we often translate as "community" or "fellowship." Paul is talking about doing life together, and all the ways that Christians should be reminding each other of the gospel on a daily basis.

Here's another way to read this verse, that brings out the meaning a little differently: "and I pray that the fellowship of your faith may become effective through the knowledge of every good thing which is in you for Christ's sake" (NASB).

If you study those two translations, it's not quite clear if Paul is saying that koinonia leads to a full understanding of Christ or that a full understanding of Christ leads to koinonia. Whenever I'm presented with an either/or like this, my answer is a resounding "Yes!" The point is that koinonia is closely connected to our experience and understanding of Christ. We can't ever divorce the two. We will miss out on "every good thing" we have in Christ if we're not "sharing" our faith, in community, in fellowship together.

This simply underscores what theologian and martyr Dietrich Bonhoeffer said in his book on community, *Life Together*: "Christianity means community through Jesus Christ and in Jesus Christ."[2] Jesus is the point. He's the goal. We glorify him by helping one another become more like him, together.

So you can see that church is more than the God-given means of providing me with companionship and friendship. (It includes that, but it's so, so much more than that.) Community is one of the primary ways we experience Christ.

To grow in connection to Christ, you need to be connected to the body of Christ, the people of God, which is the church.

2. Movement (the Bride)

When we look at the early church, we see a movement. One of the best descriptions of this is in Acts 2:42-47:

> They devoted themselves to the apostles' teaching and to fellowship, to the breaking of bread and to prayer. Everyone was filled with awe at the many wonders and signs performed by the apostles. All the believers were together and had everything in common. They sold property and possessions to give to anyone who had need. Every day they continued to meet together in the temple courts. They broke bread in their homes and ate together with glad and sincere hearts, praising God and enjoying the favor of all the people. And the Lord added to their number daily those who were being saved.

Not a semester goes by that a student doesn't come to me with this passage in mind and say, "Why don't we have that? I want that." I typically respond by saying I want that too, and that the kinds of things we see here are happening around us, if we look.

We see that the early church was a movement characterized by:
- devotion to the apostle's teaching
- devotion to fellowship, or community (koinonia, there's that word again)
- devotion to the breaking of bread—this means both the regular celebration of Communion and simply eating together regularly
- devotion to prayer—they prayed with and for each other
- the regular occurrence of miracles that filled people with awe
- a commitment to being together and meeting together for worship
- having everything in common and selling off their possessions to care for the poor
- people being saved every day

Sign me up for that! It's a beautiful picture, isn't it? It's the way the bride of Christ is supposed to look. It's in the context of this beautiful community that we experience movement. The power of the gospel and the Holy Spirit is poured out on God's gathered people, and it overflows in amazing ways. This fulfills what Jesus said in John's gospel:

> On the last and greatest day of the festival, Jesus stood and said in a loud voice, "Let anyone who is thirsty come to me and drink. Whoever believes in me, as the Scripture has said, rivers of living water will flow from within

them." By this he meant the Spirit, whom those who believed in him were later to receive. (John 7:37-39)

My point is this: if we have the Spirit, the living water, flowing from within us, it needs to go somewhere. What happens to water that doesn't move or flow? It becomes stale and stagnant. We will likewise grow stagnant if the power of God is not flowing through us to bless others. If we're not in community, the flow of living water will stagnate. We will be swamps, not streams. But when we remain open to movement, the Spirit's living water cleanses, purifies, and beautifies us, until the bride of Christ is ready for her bridegroom.

3. Growth (the Body)

Ephesians 4 is an important passage to look at when considering the body of Christ.

So Christ himself gave the apostles, the prophets, the evangelists, the pastors and teachers, to equip his people for works of service, so that the body of Christ may be built up until we all reach unity in the faith and in the knowledge of the Son of God and become mature, attaining to the whole measure of the fullness of Christ.

Then we will no longer be infants, tossed back and forth by the waves, and blown here and there by every wind of teaching and by the cunning and craftiness of people in their deceitful scheming. Instead, speaking the truth in love, we will grow to become in every respect the mature body of him who is the head, that is, Christ. From him the whole body, joined and held together by every supporting ligament, grows and builds itself up in love, as each part does its work. (Ephesians 4:11-16)

All the leaders God has given are simply to equip God's people for works of service, "so that" they can grow up. This body hasn't reached maturity—it needs to grow. While immaturity can be cute at five, it's disturbing at thirty-five, right?

Growth is necessary. Paul gives us a vivid picture of how dire our situation is if we don't grow up. We are infants, blown about and tossed around by "every wind of teaching" of cunning, crafty, and deceitful people. In other words, "Grow up and learn to swim, or you're going to die."

Remember whose body it is that we're growing into? Christ's. In Jesus and together with others, collectively we become a living display of the image of God. I need you, you need me, and we need each other, to become like Christ. Growth is a community project. To grow into who God wants us to be, we need Christ and his whole body. God draws us close to himself in Christ Jesus and closer to one another as well. Together we display the image of God and are living proof of a loving God. So when people see us, collectively, they should see Jesus. That's the church, and that's our high calling.

The Problem with Community

Unfortunately, living out our high calling as the church is easier said than done. I've heard many reasons why students don't commit to the body of Christ. Perhaps you believe some of these.

1. You've Been Hurt

What happens when you get a bunch of imperfect people together? Someone is going to get hurt. Life together is hard. It's messy. I've been hurt in community, and I've hurt others. Community means proximity. It means you're close enough to others to get hurt and to hurt them. Show me the group where no one ever has his or her feelings hurt and where there's never the need for conflict resolution, and I'll show you a group with counterfeit community where members just put on their best face and leave everyone with a superficial impression of who they really are.

Jesus uses messy diversity to change the world. Just look at his original disciples. He called Matthew, the tax collector, someone in bed with the Roman government, known for corrupt profits. He called Simon the Zealot, a political radical, dedicated to overthrowing that same government. Then he called Andrew, Peter, James, and John: a bunch of blue-collar workers with no education.

In modern terms, it may be something like an executive from Halliburton, a granola-making PETA activist, and a NASCAR pit crew all deciding to hang out and follow Jesus together. Sure, they fight sometimes. But over time their hearts are changed for each other, and Jesus uses them to change the world. Community is messy, but it's life-changing and worth the risks.

Now, that's not to excuse the hurt that's been done, but the tragedy is that hurting people need community more, not less. Healing will come in the context of loving relationship, not outside of that. If you've been hurt by people in the church (I prefer saying it that way, as opposed to "hurt by *the* church"), then know that God hates that, but he still desires for you to be connected to his body. It may be hard, but it's exactly what we need. The poor alternative is no connection at all.

2. You're Too Busy

We are highly influenced by the ideal of the rugged individual. This persona has permeated the church (which should be the ultimate display of righteous connection) in the form of "Jesus and Me" spirituality. Jesus isn't interested in individuals alone, but in a new people, a community, a fellowship. We're not just people in a room. We're *a people*.

Community can be inconvenient. Everyone says, "I'm busy." I'm busy; you're busy; we're all busy. So we have to prioritize meaningful connection with the body amid our busy schedules. That means saying no to other things. It means we can't do it all. One reason we really can't do it all is that, spiritually speaking, we won't make it. Loners get picked off. The more isolated we are, the more vulnerable we are. That's why God designed us for community.

The superspiritual (and false) version of this is, "I'm so busy with my Christian fellowship group that the most I can do is *attend* church." It happens often. And it may have happened to you without your realizing it. Sometimes the systems and structures of our groups become so elaborate that they effectively leave out time for meaningful involvement with church. Instead of being an arm of the church, campus groups functionally replace church.

There are a few problems with that.

The first is that your fellowship group isn't a church. It doesn't function as the church, particularly in terms of leadership (biblical standards of pastors/elders and deacons), and in terms of things like the sacraments (baptism and Communion). It's also not representative of the church, in all her messy and diverse glory. You need to be hanging around kids and old folks and people your parents' age. You need to see the whole body in action. The fellowship group is an artificial, homogenized group of eighteen- to twenty-two-year-olds. As a missional strike force, gathered for the purpose of reaching your campus, it's awesome. As a replacement for the church, sorry, it doesn't cut it.

The second problem with replacing church with community group is that it sets you up with artificial expectations for what church is. I've heard of far too many students who were actively involved in a fellowship group but then completely fell off the map when it came to church post-college. "I haven't found anything like I had in college." Well of course you haven't. What you had in college was an artificial ecosystem with countless events tailored just for you. You probably won't find a church just like that (and that's probably good). Students who are involved in the life of the church as undergrads avoid what a ministry friend of mine calls "the swamp," the stagnant, stuck wandering that many Christian students find themselves in during their twenties. So get involved. Get connected. By all means, be part of a fellowship group, but not at the expense of the broader church.

3. You Won't Be Around Long

I hear this all the time, but I've encouraged students to become members of my church a month before they graduate, because even if they move, they have a home church, and they know better what to look for in a new church. I've known a good number of students who start saying, "I won't be here long," in their freshman and sophomore years . . . and then, when they're seniors, kick themselves for not getting connected earlier. Angie, in her final year, told me: "After living here for almost three years I finally feel like I have a place where I belong. I have grown so much in this past year and it is because of our campus ministry and the people I have met by being a part . . . God has truly blessed my life more than I could have ever imagined this past year."

4. You're Not "Getting" Enough Out of Church

When you come to church as a consumer, mentally assessing everything from the welcome to the worship to the preaching to the cleanliness of the bathrooms, you're asking, "What can I get out of this?" The better question is, "What can I give to this? Who can I love? Serve? Welcome?" If you want to be welcomed, be a welcoming person. If you want to experience encouragement, start by encouraging others. If we do that, we won't need to worry about being welcomed and accepted and befriended.

We are meant to be a community where we are known and know each other, bearing one another's burdens (Galatians 6:2), praying with and for each other, and giving and serving together.

The Power of Body Life

Once we've dealt with our objections to life in the body, and made our commitment to participate, we can experience the power and beauty of what God has designed it to be. I love how Paul describes the body by saying that we are people "speaking the truth in love" (Ephesians 4:15). Most of us want to only do part of this. We like to be right, so we speak the truth, but often without love. Or we like to be liked, so we speak in love, even if it's without truth. But Christians are people with the grace, strength, and courage to do both of these. If we're not regularly speaking the truth in love, we will not grow into maturity. So we need to love each other enough to speak truth. Love each other enough to say hard things. Love each other enough to risk momentary discomfort for the greater goal of growth. That means we need to be willing to do this and to receive it.

Truth-telling in love is not always pleasant at the time, but it's always good. This is part of our growth. It's part of our healing. It's tempting to think that the person speaking truth in love is hurting us, when in reality they're simply exposing the wound that's already there, so it can be healed. This speaking the truth in love is how the body becomes whole, becomes well, becomes healthy.

Paul continues on in Ephesians 4:16: "From him the whole body, joined and held together by every supporting ligament, grows and builds itself up *in love*, as each part does its work" (emphasis added).

The body builds itself up, and when it does, it's unlike anything else. It can save a life. I think about a student I knew who struggled with suicidal thoughts and checked himself into the hospital. When the crisis hit, many people in the body (who already knew him and cared for him) rallied around him. They visited him, cared for him, came alongside him, and offered friendship, counsel, and care "in love." So many of us visited him that the hospital staff had a hard time figuring out how we were related. They assumed we were all family—which we are. When it was over, this student even said, "This—my church family—is my true family." That's the body of Christ, building itself up in love.

Remember that it's in Jesus that we are empowered to love one another. When it's hard, remember that Jesus gives us supernatural power to do this. Remember that it is the "whole body" that is growing and building itself up. We need everyone on board. We need to be together, and we need everyone taking responsibility. We're lacking if one part of the body is missing. One part of the body by itself can't do very much. But together, when "each part does its work," it's amazing what we can accomplish. You've heard the expression "The whole is greater than the sum of its parts"? This is truer with the Body of Christ than anything else.

The church is an essential but not exclusive sphere of God's kingdom work. It is in her and through her that you are connecting, growing, and moving in life-giving ways. The church is spiritual family. It's the home base that is separate from the other spheres that we'll look at; yet it shapes us and strengthens us for faithful engagement in them. So love the church and get involved.

CHAPTER 9

SCRIPTURE STUDY: Ephesians 4:11-16; Acts 2:42-47

Discussion Questions

1. What's your attitude toward the church? If you haven't played an active role in your church yet, what prevents you from doing so?

2. Which metaphor for church—building, bride, or body—resonates with you? Why?

3. How has Christian community led to a fuller understanding of your life with God?

4. Are you also surrounding yourself with people who are different from you? Why should churches avoid becoming "affinity groups"—gatherings of people who think and like the same things?

5. Christ loves the church—the often awkward, broken, and embarrassing bride—enough to claim her as his own. How might you grow in love for the church (God's people)?

TEN RELATIONSHIPS

"The LORD God said, 'It is not good for the man to be alone. I will make a helper suitable for him'" (Genesis 2:18). While Adam is surrounded by an untainted world, by lots of cool animals, by God himself, before sin or brokenness had entered the world, God calls it "not good." God has designed us to need other people, to be in relationship. It's part of what it means to be human.

Relationships have a uniquely God-given power to shape us. The ones we form at crucial transition points in our life, including college, have an even greater ability to shape the rest of our life. It's imperative that we are able to discern how to faithfully engage our networks of family relationships, friendships, and romantic relationships. This includes thoughtfulness in everything from how often you text your parents to how to handle the hookup culture. It includes how you relate using social media, and the importance of being present with the people God has put in your life.

In classic Kuyperian thought, the family is a distinct sphere, as opposed to "relationships." But college students occupy a unique in-between zone, where most are still under the care of parents but increasingly independent of them. You remain close to your parents in many cases but rely on your friend groups as much or even more. Simultaneously, you are forming romantic relationships that have at least the potential of leading to your own families in the future. So I've combined family, friendship, and romance all under the sphere of relationships in this chapter.

Family

1. Relationships with Parents Have Always Been a Challenge

The current generation of parents is more engaged than ever before. Perhaps your parents have been deeply involved and invested in your life for as long as you can remember. This is good and bad. Many colleges, for the first time, have had to start special programs for parents, and even install "Parent Bouncers" during move-in weekend, to get parents out of the way.

So while some of you may have the more traditional parent problems—they're too distant, too aloof, and they don't understand you or your life or your problems; many of you also have this newer problem of overinvolved parents—they don't understand that you need your space, you need room to grow up, and they can't always fix everything for you. Perhaps you even have "helicopter parents," swooping in at the slightest sign of trouble.

2. Relationships with Parents Reveal Our Hearts

No matter what your parents are like, how you relate to them is really important. Paul writes:

Furthermore, just as they did not think it worthwhile to retain the knowledge of God, so God gave them over to a depraved mind, so that they do what ought not to be done. They have become filled with every kind of wickedness, evil, greed and depravity. They are full of envy, murder, strife, deceit and malice. They are gossips, slanderers, God-haters, insolent, arrogant and boastful; they invent ways of doing evil; *they disobey their parents*; they have no understanding, no fidelity, no love, no mercy. Although they know God's righteous decree that those who do such things deserve death, they not only continue to do these very things but also approve of those who practice them. (Romans 1:28-32 emphasis added; see also 2 Timothy 3:1-5)

God takes obedience seriously and has these commands: "Honor your father and your mother, so that you may live long in the land the LORD your God is giving you" (Exodus 20:12). It's also, as Paul says, the first commandment with a promise. "Children, obey your parents in the Lord, for this is right. 'Honor your father and mother'—which is the first commandment with a promise—'so that it may go well with you and that you may enjoy long life on the earth'" (Ephesians 6:1-3). And finally, "Children, obey your parents in everything, for this pleases the Lord" (Colossians 3:20).

Now we know parents have a tremendous role in shaping us early in life. But many of us are naive to how crucial our parental relationships during the college years are for shaping our future. A lot of us think that when we get to college, we can just run from the family drama and not deal with it anymore. There's truth to this; sometimes college is a respite. Things can improve dramatically during college, it seems—but that may just be a function of not seeing each other as much, rather than actual healing. You always realize this a few days into break, right? You think you've grown up and things are better, but a few skirmishes about your late nights or cleaning your room, and what happens? You might as well be fifteen again, the way you're acting.

Many of us have serious hurts that we can't just walk away from. Generational sin—those sin patterns that are passed down from one generation to another, like a bad inheritance—is real and goes very deep. Anything that is not honoring toward parents will reap negative consequences later on. "God cannot be mocked. A man reaps what he sows" (Galatians 6:7). Hatred, resentment, irritation, and fear toward your parents will come out eventually. Often, you'll do the same thing your parents did, and freak out "I'm becoming my mom!" It won't go well with you if you don't honor your parents.

Healing comes through two unpopular words: "Honor" and "Obey." Honor is the act of recognizing the good things they have done—the sacrifices, kindness, and multitude of ways they have loved you. Even if you have to look hard. Treat them with respect even if they don't deserve it. Extend forgiveness even if they haven't asked for it. That's grace, and parents need it too.

As you get older, or if you are forced to move back home because of student loans and lack of jobs, this honor/obedience relationship will change, but it is never removed. We honor our parents until the day we die.

Your parents don't understand you. But you don't understand them either. Here are some areas where we can choose to honor them.

Control Issues. As you get older, it can be hard for your parents to understand that you are growing up, need space, and need to take responsibility for things. Too many parents intervene in students' lives: scheduling their classes, resolving conflict with their roommates, and more. Honor your parents by gently reminding them that you are getting older and are capable of handling these things. Ask for advice, not for them to be "The Fixer."

Trust Issues. Are you worthy of trust? Trust isn't just given; it's earned. Part of growing up is showing your parents that you are ready to take even more responsibility for your own welfare than they have. Your parents are asking, "Can you be trusted with yourself?" During my freshman year, my parents gave me my first ATM card. I had access to an account with spending money that was supposed to last me for the whole year. I used it all up by December. My parents were gracious, but I had to learn about not overspending and keeping track of things. I had to demonstrate that they could trust me to handle money wisely.

Differing Expectations. So much of parent-student tension involves expectations during school breaks. That first fall break or Thanksgiving break can be an epic failure. Suddenly things that were assumed, like being home for dinner, are up for grabs. You're on a completely different schedule now (what I like to call CST, College Standard Time), and it's disorienting to your parents. You're sleeping in. Maybe you don't jump to do things around the house that you used to do. Things are probably different now that you're in college. Some things probably should be. But honor your parents by being an adult and initiating a conversation about expectations.

3. Abba, Father!

Now, all parents disappoint. Even the best, most intentional, most hardworking, sincere parents fail. Whether absentee or a helicopter parent, we've all been sinned against. That's why it's so essential that we understand that God is our Father, the perfect Father.

The Spirit you received does not make you slaves, so that you live in fear again; rather, the Spirit you received brought about your adoption to sonship. And by him we cry, "Abba, Father." The Spirit himself testifies with our spirit that we are God's children. (Romans 8:15-16)

This Father will heal our hurts. Instead of cursing and condemnation, he offers perfect love, combined with perfect knowledge and understanding of who you are. God desires a growing relationship of closeness, protection, and care; but he never smothers you. He doesn't need to get anything out of you. He loves you as you are and delights in your successes. He's not needy; he's God.

Friends and Roommates

I had high hopes for friendships my freshman year. I was rooming with my high school friend, Jim. We grew up in the same neighborhood and had a lot in common: the same group of friends, classes, and interests. On our drives to high school during senior year, we talked about all the fun we would have when we got to school.

Then we arrived on campus. New freshmen arrived on Thursday, but classes didn't start until the following Wednesday. That left a lot of time to learn the campus. Everyone was hanging out, having a blast . . . except Jim. He wasn't enjoying it. He wasn't sleeping well. He was hardly eating. He seemed really stressed. On Sunday, he told me that he needed to go home, to get away for a bit. On Monday, he took the bus home. I thought he would be back for the start of class, but he wasn't. He came back a week later, but only to pack up his things. He moved back home, without taking one class. He enrolled somewhere else, and last I heard, he's done just fine. I was disappointed, but it may have been the best thing for me. Jim leaving forced me to look beyond my high school friends. It compelled me to find a Christian group, where I connected instantly. Those people remain some of my closest friends to this day.

If you're human, you can relate to the promise and pleasure of friendship, as well as the disappointment, hurt, and pain of friendships gone awry. College students find themselves in a unique phase of life, navigating stressful relationship problems for the first time—or the umpteenth time. See if you can relate to any of these issues listed on a college advice website[1]:

- First-year student needs help developing good friendships
- Help, I've been sexiled by my new roommate
- How to tell your nosy roommate to step off
- How can I tell my roommate that he smells without ruining our living situation?

People today are lonelier than ever. While twenty years ago most people had four to five close friends, nearly a quarter of people surveyed now say they have zero close friends with whom to discuss personal matters. And more than half named two or fewer confidants, most often immediate family members.

That's right, despite our email, cellphones, chatting, blogging, texting, and more, we are not more connected than ever, we are less. We may be surrounded by people, but are they really friends?

So let's talk about faithfulness in the context of friendship. We need to, because the word "friend" has become vague and confusing. Remember *The Social Network*, the story of Mark Zuckerberg? Its tagline was, "You don't get to five hundred million friends without making a few enemies." Of course, Zuckerberg doesn't actually have five hundred million friends. More than a few reviewers said that only a person who doesn't understand real friendship calls a social media contact a friend. But that's not just Zuckerberg—that's us too. We aren't sure what friendship is. We're substituting the counterfeit for the real thing. And it's not only amplifying all the brokenness of relationships but also normalizing it. I'm no technophobe—I'm on most of the social networks out there, to some degree—but I share the concern that the more we're relating online, the less we know about genuine friendship. Proverbs says something that I believe is extremely relevant to how college students approach friendship: "Do not forsake your friend or a friend of your family, and do not go to your relative's house when disaster strikes you—*better a neighbor nearby than a relative far away*" (Proverbs 27:10, emphasis added).

This verse affirms that it's good to maintain existing friendships, but that you need friends who are close by. Proximity is an important part of friendship. Before everyone had cell phones and was on Facebook, this was assumed. When you went to college, you left behind your old friends by necessity. You were content to reconnect over breaks, and slowly but surely your friends changed . . . and you changed. Now, I see students trying to be everywhere, but they're really nowhere. You're a mile wide but an inch deep.

We need help navigating life from those who are near us. As you depend on them, you become better friends. Why does Proverbs say not to go to your brother but to go to your neighbor? Because it's unwise to only have friends who are far away. Form friends here. Grow where you're planted. I talk to so many students who are lonely, "I don't really have any friends here at school; that's why I go home." And the cycle deepens.

Friendship is a ministry of presence. It is being fully here and fully present for someone. It is serving, caring for, and investing in others. I saw a powerful example of this through my friend, Alex. He was a fifth-year senior, and my roommate, Jeff, and I were mere sophomores. We were still young punks who had a lot of growing up to do, while Alex was one of the leaders of our fellowship group. In his fifth year, Alex had seen most of his peers graduate and move on. He could have mentally and socially moved on, as well. But instead of blowing off his last year as a "transition season," Alex doubled down and invested in Jeff and me. He had lived off campus for years, but he made it a point to spend tons of time with us in our tiny dorm room, in an area of campus mostly populated by freshmen. He humbled himself and went beneath himself in order to befriend us. He often slept on our ratty old loveseat instead of going home at night, so that we could spend a few more hours playing video games and talking. He ministered powerfully to us that year, through his words, but especially through his presence. To this day, it's one of the most powerful examples of incarnational ministry that I've ever experienced.

What makes a good friend? Let's look at some of the ways Proverbs describes friendship, both the kind of friend to look for and the kind of friend to be. This is wisdom about friendship that is still applicable in the age of Facebook:

1. **A friend sticks with you**. "A friend loves at all times, and a brother is born for a time of adversity" (Proverbs 17:17).

2. **A friend gives you good advice**. "Perfume and incense bring joy to the heart, and the pleasantness of a friend springs from their heartfelt advice" (Proverbs 27:9).

3. **A friend hurts you good**. "Wounds from a friend can be trusted, but an enemy multiplies kisses" (Proverbs 27:6). A friend is someone who tells you what you need to hear, not necessarily what you want to hear. Even if the sparks fly, friendship has redemptive power: "As iron sharpens iron, so one person sharpens another" (Proverbs 27:17).

4. **A friend acts with integrity**. "Do not withhold good from those to whom it is due, when it is in your power to act. Do not say to your neighbor, 'Come back tomorrow and I'll give it to you'—when you already have it with you" (Proverbs 3:27-28).

5. **A friend speaks with integrity**. "Like a club or a sword or a sharp arrow is one who gives false testimony against a neighbor" (Proverbs 25:18), and "Like a maniac shooting flaming arrows of death is one who deceives their neighbor and says, 'I was only joking!'" (Proverbs 26:18-19).

6. **Friends don't take revenge**. "Do not say, 'I'll pay you back for this wrong!' Wait for the LORD, and he will avenge you" (Proverbs 20:22), and "Do not say, 'I'll do to them as they have done to me; I'll pay them back for what they did'" (Proverbs 24:29).

7. **Friends don't pick fights**. "Hatred stirs up conflict, but love covers over all wrongs" (Proverbs 10:12); "Fools show their annoyance at once, but the prudent overlook an insult" (Proverbs 12:16); "Starting a quarrel is like breaching a dam; so drop the matter before a dispute breaks out" (Proverbs 17:14); and "It is to one's honor to avoid strife, but every fool is quick to quarrel" (Proverbs 20:3).

8. **Good friends are mere reflections of the one true friend**. "A man of many companions may come to ruin, but there is a friend who sticks closer than a brother" (Proverbs 18:24, ESV). Who does all these things

perfectly? Jesus, our older brother in the family of God, the one who sticks closer to us than even the most loyal brother.

Sex and Dating

If there's one area of relationships where we need help living faithfully, it's sex and dating. While the Bible has a good deal to say about sex, if you look in the Bible for dating, you won't find it. That doesn't mean the Bible doesn't have anything to say on the subject, however. There are many pertinent principles to guide us.

God wants us to approach romantic relationships in the same way we approach other relationships: to love wisely, selflessly, and well. He calls us to a Christlike love and a love that surrenders our will to God, letting him call the shots in our relationships. Some of us want romantic relationships way too much. We feel empty and alone, pathetic without that boyfriend or girlfriend on our arm. And some of us don't desire them enough. We are extremely phobic, fearful, turned off to relationships. God says relationships are good, and we need to be open to whatever God gives us—but in his timing, not ours.

Still, it's hard to know how to be faithful in this area. The typical ways of dating or "friends with benefits" or "hooking up" or living together aren't biblical or smart. They seem fun, but they increase the hurt and the pain. Paul wrote many helpful words to the Corinthian church about sex.

> Flee from sexual immorality. All other sins a person commits are outside the body, but whoever sins sexually, sins against their own body. Do you not know that your bodies are temples of the Holy Spirit, who is in you, whom you have received from God? You are not your own; you were bought at a price. Therefore honor God with your bodies. (1 Corinthians 6:18-20)

Honor God with Your Bodies

Here are a couple of things to keep in mind as we seek to honor God with our bodies:

1. Don't pursue a romantic relationship until the right time.

Love and sex are really powerful. I don't think we know what we are messing with. In his love song, Solomon offers this warning, "Do not arouse or awaken love until it so desires." In case we missed it, he says this three times (Song of Songs 2:7; 3:5; 8:4). Wait until it's the right time.

So when is the right time? The short answer is, when you are ready for it—when your character and commitments can match your desires. The reason for God's design for sex within marriage is not to kill your joy. It's to save you from pain and regret. Sex is complete intimacy with another person. It is sharing yourself and becoming one with another. It is the most vulnerable thing you can do. To save us from shame and guilt, God has set it up that we commit ourselves fully to one other person within marriage before we share sexual intimacy. That way, we are not compartmentalizing sex away from the other areas of our lives. To be one with someone sexually, we should also be one with that person spiritually, emotionally, relationally, physically, financially, and in every other way.

What we see in the Bible is that sexual relationships, within God's design, are good, beautiful, shame-free, guilt-free, pleasurable, fulfilling, life-giving, joy-inducing, and all-around awesome! We wouldn't have an entire book, the Song of Songs, devoted to the beauty and joy of married intimacy if God didn't want it to be good. But unfortunately, we are relentlessly inundated with competing messages about sex.

2. Sex outside of marriage hurts you and others.

Some people insist that sex outside of marriage is necessary because "you have to see if you're compatible." Sexual compatibility? There's no such thing. People are not born with a "style" of sex they like. Everybody learns to do it. Someone who talks about compatibility is really asking, "Are the things I learned from my previous partners compatible with the things my current partner learned from previous partners?" How much better to learn together, over time, within the complete safety of a commitment to one another! You can laugh and enjoy figuring it out together. Outside of marriage, it's fearful and scary because it's an audition. You have to perform at your best when there's no commitment. If you're not good enough, your partner could move on. That's no way to be intimate.

Many more insist that sex is more fun without all that commitment. Some people insist that cohabitation is the way to go. "We're practically married already," goes the thinking. This is combining "sexual compatibility" with "life compatibility." But cohabitation without the covenant commitment of marriage is like writing a check that you can't cash. As more people view living together as normal, they're taking on all of the risks of sharing everything without the comfort of the promise and shared commitment. Cohabiting people are far more likely: (1) to never get married; (2) to eventually get divorced if they do marry, and (3) to be less satisfied sexually than people who did not live together before they got married.

3. Sex with yourself hurts you and others.

What about masturbation? The Bible doesn't forbid masturbation per se. That means it is potentially permissible, but we have to ask, is it beneficial (1 Corinthians 6:12; 10:23)?

To answer that, we need to answer a few more questions: Can you do it from faith? Anything not from faith is considered sin (Romans 14:23). Can you do it without being controlled by it? Paul says in 1 Corinthians 6:12 that everything is permissible, "but not everything is beneficial" and "I will not be mastered by anything." Can you do it without lusting? Lust is sin. Jesus says:

> You have heard that it was said, "You shall not commit adultery." But I tell you that anyone who looks at a woman lustfully has already committed adultery with her in his heart. (Matthew 5:27)

Jesus says that lust is incredibly dangerous to our souls. Masturbation teaches us to have sex with ourselves, to serve ourselves, to think only of me. It teaches us to be lazy, to go instantly to physical gratification without the work of pursuing and serving another person. It teaches us not to serve and seek the pleasure of another person. It can be addicting as well. The more we do it, the more we can rewire our brain and body to get off from self-stimulation.

Porn is the same way. Its goal is to stimulate the sexual desire of someone not our spouse, which is clearly lust. Whether it is erotic images or erotic words, those ideas, images, and expectations will be embedded deep in our minds. We'll take that into bed with us. Over time, it could limit our ability to be aroused by our future spouse. And it's not victimless: pornography prostitutes and exploits millions of people (including children) around the world. Its prevalence and profitability leads to greater and greater perversions. The world thinks everything I've just told you is laughable and ridiculous, and that our desires are natural. But a redeemed view of sexuality teaches us that we are more than animals, therefore we don't have to behave like them. We don't have to follow every urge, instinct, and appetite. Not all desires are good in a fallen world, and not all should be indulged whenever we feel like it. We are human beings; we are capable of reflection and self-control. We can "say 'No' to ungodliness and worldly passions" (Titus 2:12).

How to Pursue a Relationship

So if you're committed to avoiding the corruptions of sex on your campus, how can you pursue relationships faithfully? Here are a few ideas:

1. **Don't make a relationship the be-all end-all of your existence.** Be content, and be open to God's timing. Being single is a time of great opportunities to serve in ways that you won't be able to later on. Singleness is a gift. Don't look for the gift receipt—use it. Experience the positives on this side of the fence.

2. **Know the difference between friendship and intimacy.** Get to know each other side-by-side as well as face-to-face. Serve and do things that help you get to know each other, before jumping to intimacy. Don't just watch movies . . . in the dark . . . on the couch . . . late at night.

3. **Treat all non-spouses as sisters and mothers, brothers and fathers.** Love them in that way.

4. **Be inclusive, not exclusive: don't just pair off and disappear.** Some of that is OK and appropriate if you're moving into relationship, but don't isolate yourselves. Groups are great.

5. **Ask God if you're ready to pursue a serious relationship.** Ask older, wiser people who know you if you're ready. Check your motives.

6. **Don't steal pleasures and privileges of marriage without making the commitment.** You can do this emotionally as well as physically.

7. **Take things slowly, but be intentional.** Be honest. Be cautious, especially in physical areas. Make sure your affection doesn't become foreplay. Don't do things that leave one or both of you frustrated and charged up. And in case you're wondering: oral sex and mutual masturbation count as having sex outside of marriage. You're sharing your nakedness and giving parts of yourself to another.

8. **Continually ask, "Am I loving this person?** Am I helping this person get closer to Jesus? If our future spouses were here, would they be mad?"

What If the Relationship Ends?

Even if the relationship ends, your obligation to love and care for the other person doesn't end. You are made in God's image, and so is that person. And how you handle this breakup impacts both of your souls. You owe each other love. "Let no debt remain outstanding, except the continuing debt to love one another, for whoever loves others has fulfilled the law" (Romans 13:8).

When a relationship ends, we should ask if we owe the other person anything. Do we owe this person:

- An apology?
- An explanation?

- A resolution of conflict?
- Money, or an object?

All relationships are *Coram Deo,* "in the presence of God." He has designed relationships for our mutual growth, even the hard ones. He has done this so that we will seek him.

God's not only the source but also the destination of our relationships. Whether parental, friendly, or romantic, they are all vastly incomplete. This is by design. The joys and frustrations of our relationships are meant to be signposts. They take our longings and point us to the ultimate relationship in Jesus Christ. Like Paul says when talking about marriage, "This is a profound mystery—but I am talking about Christ and the church" (Ephesians 5:32). Jesus is the ultimate relationship, the goal of all our other relationships.

CHAPTER 10

**SCRIPTURE STUDY: Read the Proverbs passages
listed in this chapter.**

Discussion Questions

1. Are your relationships with Christians different than those with non-Christians? In what ways? Should they be?

2. Parents, friends, and romantic relationships: Which is most difficult for you right now? Which relationship is thriving? Why?

3. How present are you in your relationships? Are you accountable to and intentional with others? What are ways to prevent yourself from becoming a mile wide and an inch deep?

4. Write down the name of someone you could you love and honor better. List three steps that will help you do this.

ELEVEN ACADEMICS AND WORK

For a college student, academic study is your main work. This is important, because work is a gift of God. It's part of how he's designed us. It's one of the ways we reflect his image. God worked for six days, then rested. God declared his work "good," and his purpose for our work is that it be good as well. Work that is for God gives us purpose, focus, and joy. Our work is designed to be a way we can know Jesus better. Our work, in academics, is knowledge work, and that knowledge is never meant to be separated from Jesus, "in whom are hidden all the treasures of wisdom and knowledge" (Colossians 2:3).

But work is also hard. Work is subject to the curse of sin. There are "thorns and thistles" that frustrate our efforts, as any student in that weed-out organic chemistry course can tell you. There are those annoying GenEd requirements . . . and the stupid assignments . . . and the professors who are totally unreasonable and unfair . . . not to mention the hassle of getting to that 8 a.m. class on Monday morning.

If you're like most students, you have a love-hate relationship with your studies. You love certain things you study. You love learning new things, creating new things, gaining knowledge and skills and confidence in a subject you enjoy. But there's also a lot to dislike. For better and for worse, our academic work occupies our minds and our time, and shapes the work that we will do for the rest of our lives (even if, like many people, you end up working in a field unrelated to your major).

So how should we approach this area of our lives, one that is, after all, the stated reason for why we're in college in the first place? Faithful engagement in our academic work means avoiding the converse mistakes of caring about it too little and caring about it too much. On one hand, we shouldn't be OK with being lazy or lackadaisical about our studies. But on the other hand, we need to be careful that we are not turning academic success into an idol. Both are common among college students. Let's start by putting academics in its rightful place.

Academic Idolatry

I meet too many students who justify their idolatry of academic achievement by saying, "I'm here to be a student, first and foremost." If they want to spiritualize it, they'll say, "God brought me here to be a student." That sounds pious, and parents undoubtedly love hearing how serious you are about your studies. But let me ask you some questions: Are you going to be a student for the rest of your life? Is it the most important thing about you, even in college? Is that your identity? No. It's something you're doing, but it's not your being. You are a Christian, first and foremost. Being a Christian comes before any of your doing.

Have you considered the fact that life-wide faithfulness may not mean getting straight A's? Doing what God wants in every area of your life may not mean reaching your highest academic potential—and that's OK. In seminary, I had a professor, the late Al Groves, who was famous for how he started his class on the first day. He would say, "Most of you will not get an A in this class. This class is hard, it is demanding, and A-level work can only happen if you don't have other commitments. So if you have a job, you need to work. That takes time. You should also be serving in your church somehow. That takes time. If you're married, and if you have kids, you need to love your spouse and love your kids. That all takes time. If, however, you don't have any of those things, and are independently wealthy, single, and uninvolved in church, then you might get an A."

I was poor, married, and involved in my church. I got a B. It was one of the best B's I ever got.

We need to ask what the real goal of our academic striving is. Why do we want the A's? What's the goal?

- Is it to get on the dean's list, to get an asterisk and some Latin phrase after our name in the graduation program?
- Is it to land the best internship and then the best job and then to make mad loot and pay off all our debt and drive a sweet car in an amazing house in Malibu?
- Maybe our goal is "knowledge for knowledge's sake." Knowledge is good, but wisdom is better, and God is the source of both.

Let's say you get straight A's. Let's say you gain recognition, financial success, or a head filled with knowledge. So what? To paraphrase Jesus, what good is it to gain the whole (academic) world, yet forfeit your soul?

Knowledge is from God and is meant to draw us back to him, not away from him. The danger is that we turn from our love of the Creator and worship created things instead (Romans 1:25). We can be so enamored with what we're studying (or what we hope to get from our studies) that we begin to squeeze God out. We may go to church or read our Bible occasionally, but in our hearts' holy of holies, we've begun to nudge God out. God's version of academic success is different from ours. God gave us capabilities and opportunities in academics not to further our own little kingdoms but to play our part in expanding his. He gave us a brain so that we would know him and his creation better. Eternally speaking, the tragic irony of academic idolatry is that no matter how much we know or how much success we have, if we leave God out, we've missed the point. We may be among the experts in the world on our particular subject, but if we don't know God, we're fools.

Unrenewed Minds

While knowledge isn't to be worshiped, we must still be faithful in our studies. I have a friend who teaches New Testament and ancient Near East studies at a public university. Because of her content, she gets a high percentage of Christians in her classes. And she dreads them. Now, she is not hostile toward Christianity—far from it. There are professors who go out of their way to attack Christians and help them "unlearn" everything they have been taught, but she's not one of them. Her classroom is one that presents the current scholarship on early Christianity—some of which lines up with Bible-believing, evangelical Christianity and some of which does not. Presenting it doesn't mean she's taking a position or trying to destroy someone's faith. It means she's doing her job.

But a certain subset of loudly self-identified Christians take it upon themselves to fight anything that doesn't match up with their rudimentary understanding of scholarly subjects, like textual criticism, form criticism, ancient historiographical practices, and more. They loudly contradict such points in argumentative, disruptive ways. They protest by sighing loudly, slouching in their seats and crossing their arms. If really provoked, they make a point of grandstanding and even walking out in the middle of class. If they get a grade they don't like, they accuse my professor friend of religious discrimination in angry emails to the dean. They justify this behavior as being faithful. And hardly ever do they make their point through a well researched, meticulously-crafted term paper. It's a sad day when the classes on Christianity are populated by Christians who make the most noise and do the least work.

Throughout our lives we will hear ideas that run contrary to the truth. We should expect that in this world. Even if we're (partially) right, what good is winning the argument if we've turned everyone within hearing distance off to Jesus? How you say something matters just as much as what you say. As 1 Peter 3:15 commands, we should speak in gentleness, not anger. We must show respect, not rudeness. We must keep a clear conscience, not saying or doing anything we would regret. Disagreeing with a professor does not excuse us to do shoddy academic work. Instead of brooding, write a good paper. Make a good argument. I find it tragically ironic that the people who want everyone to know how much they care about Jesus can be such bad witnesses in the classroom. Their poor work and their attitudes aren't doing Jesus any favors, and it's not pleasing to him, either.

This scenario of encountering teaching we view as contrary to our faith is but one example of students justifying their laziness. Christian students aren't alone in this. The previously mentioned book *Academically Adrift* found that today's college students spend less time studying than any previously studied generation. The authors of the study found that today's students use only 9 percent of their time for studying, while spending 51 percent on socializing and recreation. They write, "The portrayal of higher education emerging from [this study] is one of an institution focused more on social than academic experiences. Students spend very little time studying, and professors rarely demand much from them in terms of reading and writing."[1]

Christians ought to be the last ones coasting by or slacking off. By not working hard or doing things well, we reflect poorly on Jesus and his church. We treat our work as something to be avoided, instead of honoring Jesus with it.

Some of us are pretty far from the angry, protesting Christian I just described. We're more the person who *never* speaks up, the undercover Christian. Classmates and professors may never even know that our faith shapes everything we believe (assuming it does). Often, we're afraid to identify as a Christian in the classroom because we are uninformed. We've never taken it upon ourselves to understand why we believe what we do. We've never thought about how to communicate it to people who don't believe or who may even be hostile to belief. No wonder people have unfavorable impressions of the Christian faith. We often don't make the best case.

Friends, this should not be. There is, unfortunately, a powerful strain of anti-intellectualism running through the church, one that creates a false dichotomy between head and heart, brains and spirituality. This dualistic way of thinking ignores the fact that Jesus is extremely concerned with the life of your mind. What you think, how you think, and what you believe—it all belongs to God. It is all meant to be sacrificed to him.

> I appeal to you therefore, brothers [and sisters], by the mercies of God, to present your bodies as a living sacrifice, holy and acceptable to God, which is your spiritual worship. Do not be conformed to this world, but be transformed by the renewal of your mind, that by testing you may discern what is the will of God, what is good and acceptable and perfect. (Romans 12:1-2, ESV)

To worship is, in part, to be transformed by the renewing of our minds. The problem isn't that non-Christians think "faith" and "mind" are opposites, that we turn our brains off when we become Christians. The problem is that so many Christians believe this. It couldn't be more false. So how can we faithfully engage our studies in a way that honors God?

Academic Faithfulness

Understand the Academic Side of Christianity

Christianity is much more than head knowledge. But it's not less than head knowledge. To be faithful in the classroom, for our own growth and for our witnesses to others, we need to become familiar with the academic and intellectual side of Christianity. Sometimes students will say, "I don't need to explain or know all that stuff. No amount of persuasion or arguing by me will change their minds." True, you and I can't argue anybody into knowing Jesus. But God uses all means—people, books, and timely conversations. Here are some ways we can study up:

Learn your Bible. Where do you turn when you're sitting in a religious studies class and the professor states that Jesus never claimed to be God? Do you have some verses on hand? Do you know that Jesus claimed divinity every time he said, "I AM" in the Gospels, especially in John? Can you pull up any of the claims Christ made that only God can fulfill: forgiving people's sins; allowing people to worship him; being the way, the truth, and the life of God; giving his life as a ransom for all of humanity; rising from the dead? There are no new arguments against Christianity. If you want to know the best answers, learn what's in your Bible.

Learn *about* your Bible. Do you know how to respond when the guy down the hall says the Bible is just a collection of stories compiled by mistaken Christians hundreds of years later? Do you know why the Bible can be trusted? Do you know how manuscript evidence gives more credence to the Bible than any other ancient document? Can you describe why it's the inspired Word of God? Or for that matter, can you explain why it's OK for Christians to eat shellfish? It will come up in conversation, I guarantee.

Learn some history. Christianity gets slandered all the time. Whenever possible, set the record straight. But when it's true, own it. For example, when people claim that Christianity is inherently racist, it's worth talking about William Wilberforce and the other evangelicals of the Clapham sect who were at the very forefront of the abolitionist movement. It's worth talking about why the slaves in the US so quickly adopted Christianity and found it so liberating. Or how the vast majority of Christians in the world today are in the global South and have dark skin.

For every accusation that has some merit (the role of Christianity in the Crusades or the Salem Witch Trials, for example), I'm continually astounded at other things that get laid at the feet of the church. If the Nazis were somehow Christian, then what was Dietrich Bonhoeffer doing in a concentration camp? Distinguish between genuine Christianity and people who appropriate, steal, and twist it for nefarious reasons.

Read theology, apologetics, and books on worldview. Part of renewing our minds is understanding more of why we believe what we believe. Two great, accessible introductions to theology are J. I. Packer's *Concise Theology* and Wayne Grudem's *Bible Doctrine*. In the area of developing a Christian worldview, I recommend *Creation Regained*, by Al Wolters; *What Is a Christian Worldview?* by Philip Graham Ryken; *Your Mind's Mission*, by Greg Jao; *The Universe Next Door*, by James Sire; *Total Truth* by Nancy Pearcey; and *Rethinking Worldview*, by J. Mark Bertrand. My friends Don Opitz and Derek Melleby also have a great book-length treatment of the ideas we're talking about in this chapter, called *The Outrageous Idea of Academic Faithfulness*.

In the area of apologetics, consider not only C. S. Lewis's *Mere Christianity* but also *Miracles*, his works on suffering in *The Problem of Pain* and *A Grief Observed*, and his many short essays. I'm of the opinion that Lewis's best work may be his fiction, including *Perelandra*, the second book in his Space Trilogy. Tim Keller's *The Reason for God* is a thoughtful, carefully reasoned, and extremely practical work making the case for Christianity. *The Case for . . .* series by Lee Strobel answers many of the most common questions that college students have, in a very accessible interview format. These are just a few of many excellent resources related to understanding and defending your faith. But this is at most only half of our task. We also need to understand the Christian side of our field(s) of study.

Understand the Christian Side of (Your Corner of) Academia

As a Christian student, it's imperative that you learn about your major/field of study from a Christian perspective. Apart from God, the world tends toward disorder and fragmentation. Things break from their moorings and break apart from each other. As Christians we view all truth as God's truth, and so we pursue the reintegration of all knowledge under God. This means looking with God-designed lenses at our field and asking, "What did they get right? What is true in this? What reflects God's design? Where is common grace evident? What did they borrow from God?"

It also means doing a little research into Christian thinkers and achievers in your field. What have they written? How have they handled the most difficult issues that come up? I want to emphasize, this isn't just for religion or philosophy students. We all have to know this. Whether we're in education, the sciences, fine arts, liberal arts, or something else, there are Christians who have gone before us in our particular fields of study. Find out who they are. Learn from them. Soak up their wisdom.

Of course, this takes a little more work. I'm going to encourage something that you might think is ridiculous: "double study." Essentially, working first to understand your subject, then working to understand it from a Christian perspective. "What?" you ask. "I have a hard enough time with studying, let alone 'double study.'" But hear me out on this. We're talking about connecting our studies with our faith. We're talking about integrating the truth we're coming across with God's truth. We're talking about connecting our work to the work God has planned for us. We will get more out of our work if we commit to seeing it through God's eyes. This is not a zero-sum game; giving first priority to God does not make our academics suffer. The student I knew who did double study better than anyone else is now a Fulbright Scholar.

Here are a few more ways we can honor God through the renewing of our minds:

Read widely. Knowledge and understanding is God's gift. He has made an incredible world. So read well, and read widely. Don't just read spiritual junk food as you mindlessly surf the web. Read challenging books, magazines, and articles. Read across a variety of genres. Read things that you aren't assigned to read. If you like fiction, throw in some nonfiction (and vice versa).

Study as worship. Approach your studies as an act of worship. Do this consciously. Make it your habit to pray for God to reveal himself to you as you go to class or the library. Expect him to do it. I'll never forget an encounter I had with God in BiSci 003. It was a GenEd requirement and, while I hated biology, I had to take the class. So I asked God to show me more of himself in the class. I remember being overcome with awe as I studied the intricacies of the endocrine system and the regulatory functions of the hypothalamic-pituitary-adrenal axis. Have you ever worshiped God for the pituitary gland? You should. I never liked biology, but when I asked God to help me understand it, it became an act of worship. Treat all your work this way.

Don't major in your ministry. Major in your major. It's often stated as a badge of honor. "I was so involved with my fellowship group, I should have majored in it." Listen, I hope you're highly involved with your church and fellowship, as we talked about in chapter 9. You should be. But faithfulness to God means faithfulness in ministry and in our studies. That means there will be things we need to say no to in both areas. Honor God in your studies. And honor him in everything else you do too.

Finally, "Whatever you do, whether in word or deed, do it all in the name of the Lord Jesus, giving thanks to God the Father through him" (Colossians 3:17). Just in case we forget, Paul says basically the same thing a few verses later: "Whatever you do, work at it with all your heart, as working for the Lord" (v. 23). It's all for God. So study, write, present, and take exams for Jesus. Do it for him, with all your heart. It's your spiritual act of worship, and it honors him when we are transformed by the renewing of our minds.

CHAPTER 11

SCRIPTURE STUDY: Romans 12:1-2; Colossians 3:17,23

Discussion Questions

1. What's your attitude toward your academic work? Do you love it? Hate it? Endure it? And why?

2. What is a Christlike response if you are in a class and are taught something different from or hostile to Christianity?

3. Do you tend to overwork or underwork? Do you worship academic accomplishment, or not value it enough?

4. How can you honor God in the classes you're currently taking?

5. What are you currently learning about that may be used for the kingdom?

TWELVE LEADING ON CAMPUS

Leadership is one of the buzzwords of campus life. Colleges build leaders. At least they aspire to. Somewhere in the websites, brochures, and tours that your college gives are some statements about how your college builds leaders, develops leaders, cultivates leaders, unlocks leadership potential, and more. And to be sure, college gives you unparalleled opportunities for developing leadership. On your campus are tons of clubs, teams, societies, organizations, and groups. I'm always amazed by involvement fairs—seemingly every activity under the sun is represented, from model railroading to astronomy, honor societies to the futurist society, snowboarding to Spanish, anime to zoology. All these groups represent places where Christians can have a redemptive, kingdom influence. And though all these groups have officers, it's important to note that simply having a title does not make someone a leader.

What makes a leader, and what kind of leadership reflects Jesus and furthers his kingdom? It's helpful to start by identifying what leadership is not. We often see true leadership being hijacked by controlling, in-it-for-themselves people. But on the other hand, we also see people never raising their hands, stepping forward, or opting in; more than content to sit on the sidelines and in the shadows, they let others do the leading, while their own gifts and abilities go unused and undeveloped. Which side do you fall on? Let's look at the controlling, power-trip side of leadership first.

Not So with You

I love this fascinating scene in Mark's gospel, where two of Jesus' disciples, James and John, approach him with a request: "We want you to do for us whatever we ask" (Mark 10:35). Has there ever been a greater combination of faith and arrogance? They believe Jesus is capable of anything they could ask or imagine, but it's all for them. They ask Jesus if they can sit next to him in glory. It's a miracle Jesus didn't strike the "Sons of Thunder" with lightning right then and there. Instead, he patiently responds, "You don't know what you are asking" (Mark 10:38). He goes on to explain that the path to glory goes through suffering, a suffering so great that they can't imagine it. Then he proceeds to teach them about the nature of leadership and how different it is from worldly definitions:

> Jesus called them together and said, "You know that those who are regarded as rulers of the Gentiles lord it over them, and their high officials exercise authority over them. Not so with you. Instead, whoever wants to become great among you must be your servant, and whoever wants to be first must be slave of all. For even the Son of Man did not come to be served, but to serve, and to give his life as a ransom for many." (Mark 10:42-45)

Jesus completely flips their understanding of leadership. They had thought that greatness, glory, and advancement would go to the ones who were most aggressive about it. They even enlisted their mother in the behind-the-scenes campaign, according to Matthew 20:20-21, something some of us can relate to. The other disciples weren't happy about this, "When the ten heard about this, they became indignant with James and John" (Mark 10:41). The Twelve were like a small fraternity—full of gossip, backstabbing, drama, and shifting alliances. The disciples are refreshingly and (scarily) familiar in their faults.

Jesus basically replies, "Wow, you really don't get it. It's the Gentiles who go for all that power-tripping, controlling, look-at-how-great-I-am status stuff. Not so with you. You should operate completely differently. Whatever you think you should be doing, flip it upside down. If you want to be great, it doesn't mean climbing the ladder, it means going to the bottom. If you want glory, don't make other people serve you, serve them. If you want a title, make it 'slave.' Do you want an example? Look no farther than me, the Son of Man." He came to serve, and to give his life as a ransom for many. He did this when he washed their feet and ultimately when he died on the cross to purchase their lives with his blood.

So let's apply this to our campus organizations. We don't need to look very far to see "Gentiles" lording their authority over others. Just look at how freshmen are treated when they join many groups. They're hazed, teased, and forced to do all the jobs no one else wants to do. The justification for this? "We had to go through it when we were freshmen; it's your turn." The authority of the senior leaders, the ones who have waited their turn and had to work their way up from the bottom, is fiercely guarded and rigidly enforced. They won't go beneath themselves, because that's what underclassmen are for. If you cross them or even question them, you pay the consequences. They don't let go of their position easily, because they've earned the power, prestige, and other perks.

So think for a minute how radical Jesus' leadership program is. He's proposing that the senior, not the freshman, step forward to be hazed. That the president of the society, not the new recruit, have to go through the humiliating ritual—again. That the BMOC clean up the vomit—of the freshman. That we should aspire to be the "little," not the "big." He's saying that the way up is down, and that the path to glory goes through humility and even suffering. Even though he's the King of the Universe and has more right than anyone to be served, he's using terms like "servant" and "slave" positively. This is not the story we usually see played out on campus.

Opting Out

It's not just power-tripping leaders who diverge from Jesus' leadership plan. Sometimes the leaders we don't have are just as harmful as the controlling, selfish leaders we do have. They don't harm us by their actions but by their inaction. What if Abraham Lincoln had stayed in private practice and never led our country? What if Martin Luther King Jr. had stayed home? If the leaders we need don't lead, we miss out on their unique contributions. Unfortunately, good leaders regularly opt out of leadership, leaving it for someone else.

Why do good leaders opt out? Some say they're too busy. They just have too much going on. But if you're not leading anywhere, you're probably trying to do too much. Understand, I'm not necessarily talking about the kind of visible, up-front, vocal positions that we often think of when we think leaders. You may not be the class president type, but you can lead in ways that fit your gifting and ability. Just don't make yourself so busy that you never get to use those gifts.

Others are too fearful to lead. This is common when you're young. It was one of the things Paul needed to encourage young Timothy about. He said, "Don't let anyone look down on you because you are young, but set an example for the believers in speech, in conduct, in love, in faith and in purity" (1 Timothy 4:12). In other words, don't worry about what other people think of you out of fear; get in the game. Lead them. He also told him: "For the Spirit God gave us does not make us timid, but gives us power, love and self-discipline" (2 Timothy 1:7). Good advice for any young leader who lacks confidence. The God who is with you, and the Spirit of God who is in you, is greater than any challenge you will face. Do not fear.

Finally, we see leaders opt out because they are too selfish. They would rather play the latest first-person shooter or surf Pinterest than spend time and energy leading others. They are often quite good at deflecting praise in false humility, which only serves to keep them out of leadership.

The point is this: We need leaders. And not just any leaders, but leaders who reflect the leadership of King Jesus. We need you to provide that on your campus. Your campus, your city, and the world needs you to lead like Jesus. So how can you become that leader? First let's talk about what leadership is.

What Leadership Is

Leadership is not a title. It's not a position. So what is it? To put it simply, leadership is influence. Influence is defined as "the action or process of producing effects on the actions, behavior, opinions, etc., of another or others." Leadership makes things happen. Leadership effects what people do, how they behave, and what they think. Leaders are influencers. You influence others. How do you use your influence? What is the effect you produce? Christlike leaders think and act with redemptive influence as the goal of their actions. Christlike leaders know that our influence is a gift and should be used to advance Christ's kingdom of reconciliation.

Our leadership is not only for Jesus but also should be like Jesus. The Christlike leader needs to regularly answer four questions: (1) Who am I? (2) What am I doing? (3) Where am I going? and (4) How am I doing it?

1. Who Am I?

This is the question for a leader's heart. This is about identity. For Christians, our identity doesn't start with, "I am a leader," or "I am a _____" (fill in title of choice). It's essential that our identity begin with, "I am a sinner saved by grace. I am an adopted and accepted child of God." Before we get to what we do, we need to remember who we are and whose we are. Our identity in Christ grounds us and gives us a foundation for the inevitable challenges that we'll face as leaders. If our character isn't based in the bedrock of Jesus, we'll be easily shaken.

The reason so many gifted leaders fall is because they skip the question of identity. They jump right to skills and techniques. They get good at making speeches, forming plans, recruiting allies, and generally doing stuff well. But skill without character is a scary thing. It's influence without heart. Without character formation, leaders become hollow, vulnerable, and enslaved to their worst instincts. That's how you get multi-billion-dollar business fraud at places like Enron or on Wall Street. People who are really good at what they do—but act in service to greed and deception.

The Christlike leader starts with this question of who am I. When we know that we are sinners saved by grace, this should create a deep and abiding humility. Christians should be exceedingly humble people. People often think that humility is the opposite of what a leader needs. They think a leader needs a certain swagger and a confidence verging on arrogance. That level of swag can get you up the ladder. But here's what's interesting: it doesn't make the best leaders. In the landmark book, *Good to Great*, Jim Collins distinguishes between Level 4 and Level 5 leaders.[1] The Level 4 leaders were highly accomplished and got results. But they created systems and structures that were all about them. They were often hard to deal with (because of their egos), and when they left (usually quickly) all the gains they had made collapsed. Level 5 leaders, on the other hand, were often characterized by humility. They didn't fill up the room with their loud or flashy personalities. They weren't even the first person to come to mind when you think leader. But they quietly and humbly led their organizations to gains that lasted long after they were gone. Humility makes for better leaders.

When we read about leadership in the Bible, we see that Christlike leaders know they haven't "arrived." When Peter addresses elders in 1 Peter 5, he includes himself in the need for instruction—and he was the apostle Peter—the guy who walked on water, was witness to the resurrection, and preached an incredible, world-changing sermon in Acts 2. If Peter was humble enough to receive instruction and correction, you and I should probably be open to it too.

A few years ago, a student named Christian Ragland approached me. He was running for president of student government at Penn State. This is a pretty prominent position on our campus. If you're president, your name and face is in the newspaper almost every day. The good presidents take it upon themselves to represent the students to the administration. And Christian was a very good president. As he entered the rigors of the election season, Christian sought me out because he knew he needed counsel, prayer, wisdom, and guidance. I couldn't tell him much about the dynamics of politics at Penn State, but we talked a lot about his heart: How to respond to anonymous attacks and slander. How to love people who didn't like him or wanted to see him fail. How to navigate being an African-American candidate at an overwhelmingly white institution. How to build bridges to student populations that might not look favorably on a Jesus-loving candidate who started nearly every day by quoting Bible verses in his Facebook status. Christian had the wisdom to tend to his heart first, and it made him a highly respected, highly influential, and highly effective leader.

We need more young leaders like this. Unfortunately, younger people have the reputation for not listening well to their elders. Nearly every week, I read articles about how employers don't know what to do with disrespectful, rude, and entitled millennials. This has probably always been the case with regard to how older generations view younger ones, but there's also some truth to it. Christian leaders—young and old—should be different. We should set a different tone: one of respect, patient listening, humility, and submission. A good leader is one who has the heart to submit to his or her leaders. We're called to do so.

> Obey your leaders and submit to them, for they are keeping watch over your souls, as those who will have to give an account. Let them do this with joy and not with groaning, for that would be of no advantage to you. (Hebrews 13:17, ESV)

Leaders are humble, humbled people. This is a humility that does not paralyze us but propels us. G. K. Chesterton put it well in calling for a return to old humility. He writes, "The old humility was a spur that prevented a man from stopping; not a nail in his boot that prevented him from going on. For the old humility made a man doubtful about his efforts, which might make him work harder. But the new humility makes a man doubtful about his aims, which will make him stop working altogether."[2]

2. What Am I Doing?

This question addresses a leader's tasks. Leaders lead. We do things, and so we have to make sure we're doing the right things. So what are you doing to lead and influence others in Christlike ways?

We learn in the Bible that one of the main tasks of leaders is to care for the people God has put around you. One of the most common metaphors of this involves shepherds and sheep. Peter says that pastors and elders—the main leaders of a church—should "shepherd the flock of God that is among you" (1 Peter 5:2, ESV). Our English word "pastor" is from the Latin word for "shepherd," and Jesus calls himself the Good Shepherd in John 10. So, to lead like Jesus means to care for the flock as Jesus did: to feed, guide, and protect. Even to lay down your life for the sheep. Think Psalm 23. It also means the willingness to break up some fights and clean up some messes. Leadership is signing up to take on other people's problems. This is where humility becomes so important. It takes humility for a leader to wade through the mess.

I'll never forget one of the most vivid leadership lessons I've ever seen. During my summers in college, I worked on the grounds crew of a golf course. My boss was a deacon at my church. People liked working for him because he was good, reasonable, and fair. One day, during our early morning mowing of the putting greens, one of my coworkers came back to report he had found something interesting on one of the greens. The night before, some neighborhood kids had partied on the course, leaving beer cans and trash all around. This wasn't anything new. But they had also left behind something else. I believe the exact words were, "There's number 2 in the hole on number 13." Ewww. Now Sumner, my boss, would have had every right at that moment to tell any of us: "Go get some gear and clean up that mess." We were just summer employees— he had advanced degrees in golf course management. We were just college kids, and he was the boss. He had important things to do, and we were just hired help. But instead of making one of us do it, Sumner grabbed some gear and cleaned out hole number 13—thankfully before any golfers got there. He did it because he was a humble leader and because he loved the course more than any of us did. That's leadership.

Years later, I was reminded of this while doing what we called "toilet evangelism." On Saturday mornings, our Christian group would head to student apartment complexes and offer to clean people's bathrooms to show Jesus' love to them. As we cleaned their toilets, we told them about Jesus. Shock and awe was the usual response. Sometimes I wish leadership and caring for people weren't so messy. But we need leaders to clean up the place.

No matter what kind of group we find ourselves leading, we will inevitably lead hurting people. Whether we're on the newspaper staff or leading the ballroom dancing club, God will put needy, broken people in front of us. Faithful leadership doesn't mean simply fulfilling the duties of our officer position. It means caring for those hurting people. I find it very interesting that the Bible holds caring and authority together. In many fields, authority and decision-making are supposed to be separated from caring; and caring is supposed to be fenced off from authority. Doctors need to make decisions, so they're often taught to keep their distance from their patients—as if caring compromises authority. On the flip side, people who care—such as social workers, psychologists, or counselors—are often allowed very little authority. But caring and leadership should go together. The ultimate example is Jesus. He perfectly combined authority and compassion.

3. Where Am I Going?

The question of direction zeroes in on a leader's goals and motivations. It's the question of why we lead. We must regularly check our goals to ensure that we're on a good trajectory. We must regularly consider our motives, to confirm that they are good and come from a Christlike heart.

For example, it's always good to ask ourselves if we're taking a leadership position for selfish reasons. Campus leadership positions usually aren't financially profitable, but they can profit us in other ways. It's often a temptation to take a position simply to pad our résumé. Or maybe we want power and influence over a rival or to settle a score. Motives are sneaky things. Are we trying to make ourselves a BMOC or make Jesus greater?

Checking our motives also points us to what is good and positive. We ask, "What's the point? What are we aiming for?" In our church, we talk often about connection. We aim to be people who are connected to Jesus, each other, and the world, who are in turn connecting students to Jesus, each other, and the world. That's our goal. That's our purpose. If we're not doing what God has called us to do, students lose out on Jesus. They lose out on community. They lose out on purpose. Asking "Why?" gets at the emotion and the fire of our desires. When we're feeling dry, worn out, and beaten down, reminding ourselves of the goal is energizing.

Christlike leaders keep their destination at the forefront. They exercise their holy imaginations to see, by faith, how the people and groups they lead can reflect Jesus and his kingdom. They work with the goal of blessing the people God has put around them, in every way. They bring renewal—new life, energy, and vision—to everything they touch. They seek, in Jesus' name, to redeem what has been broken, neglected, and abused. They generally work for the flourishing of their campus. Their hope and goal is to leave the campus better than when they found it.

4. How Am I Doing It?

This is a question about how leaders accomplish what they're supposed to do. Where can we make our contribution? What is significant, special, and central about our contribution as a leader? What is it that only we can do? Christlike leaders know their position. They know where they stand.

Jesus once met a centurion (a Roman military leader) who amazed him. The centurion asked Jesus to heal his servant, and Jesus offered to go to his house.

The centurion replied, "Lord, I do not deserve to have you come under my roof. But just say the word, and my servant will be healed. For I myself am a man under authority, with soldiers under me. I tell this one, 'Go,' and he goes; and that one, 'Come,' and he comes. I say to my servant, 'Do this,' and he does it."

When Jesus heard this, he was amazed and said to those following him, "Truly I tell you, I have not found anyone in Israel with such great faith." (Matthew 8:8-10)

What was Jesus amazed by? He was blown away by the faith of this Gentile who didn't lord his authority over others. The centurion recognized that he had authority, but that he was also under authority. And in the presence of Jesus, he recognized that he was under Jesus' authority. The centurion knew his place. Knowing and remembering our place before Jesus shapes our role. It shapes how we position ourselves as leaders. Like Paul, we tell those we lead, "Imitate me, as I also imitate Christ" (1 Corinthians 11:1, HCSB). Our leadership legitimacy doesn't come from ourselves; it comes from the degree to which we imitate Jesus. Ambassadors don't have any authority on their own; they only have authority to the extent that the country they represent has given it to them. We are ambassadors of Christ (2 Corinthians 5:14-21).

As imitators of Christ, leaders are pacesetters. We want people to follow our example. Our words and actions are not for our own benefit; they are for the benefit of others. We seek to be transparent so that others see Jesus in us. As imitators of Christ, we are also connectors. We seek to uncover or discover the ways in which our group's purpose can connect to God's common grace. This may be as subtle as encouraging the club we lead to make better use of our money. Or it could mean leading by example and hosting a post-meeting party that specifically does not include alcohol. It could be a sorority president working to change the environment so that people are more supportive. It could be a team captain making a point of building up everyone on the team. Whether or not we have a title, leadership is leveraging our influence to have a Christlike impact on those around us.

So What Does Leadership Look Like?

If put in a position of influence, use it! Let's take the area of athletics. On many campuses, athletics are the tail that wags the dog. Star athletes can have a powerful role in shaping the culture of a campus. When these star athletes are Christians, they can use that influence for kingdom purposes. But how should they use it?

My friend, Joe Crispin, is a professional basketball player. He's played professionally in the US and Europe for over a decade. He excelled during his college career, leading his team to the Sweet 16 in the NCAA Tournament. Joe is a scorer and a straight-up baller, fearlessly charging the lane, or dropping threes with ice in his veins. On every team he's been on, he's been a leader. He has a philosophy on how to play the game and can articulate it well. He wants to be a coach someday.

Joe is also a Christian. He became a Christian during his college career. He grew quickly in his faith, and he found that it helped him put things in perspective and deal with the ups and downs of winning and losing. When he really was a BMOC, his faith helped keep him grounded. But Joe found that his faith in Christ also did more. Some people were thrilled to hear that Joe was a Christian—"Let's get the star basketball player to give his testimony!" There's nothing wrong with that. It's a great use of influence. But Joe started to feel like that's all people wanted from him. As if the only reason he had been given the talent to play ball was to share his faith. As if the only application of his faith to basketball was to throw in a shout out to "my Lord and Savior Jesus Christ" during an interview.

Joe is a thoughtful guy. He began to ask a lot of questions about the Bible, about theology in general, and about all the ways his faith informs the way he plays. He's developed a Christian theology of competition (that I hope he writes a book on some day). In a sport that often rewards the players with the biggest egos and "me-first shoot-first" attitudes, he's thought about what it means to be on a team and be a team player. His faith shapes how hard he works, during the season and during the off-season. It's shaped how he interacts with his coaches and fellow players, causing him to look for ways to help, support, and encourage them. It's meant saying no to some opportunities, so that he can spend more time with his family. And yes, he's ready to talk about Jesus with the media, coaches, or players, when appropriate. But in all these things, he seeks to imitate Christ. In doing so, he's become a leader worth following.

CHAPTER 12

SCRIPTURE STUDY: Mark 10:35-45

Discussion Questions

1. Describe someone whose leadership has impacted you. How did they speak into your life, and why was it significant?

2. Some people are naturally assertive and controlling; others are fearful and passive. Where do you tend to fall on this spectrum, and how can you lead more like Jesus?

3. What makes someone a leader? Do you think of yourself as a leader? Why or why not?

4. Where does your campus need some godly leadership? In what ways is God calling you to lead?

THIRTEEN PARTYING AND PLEASURE

My friend Garrett Hawk leads the Christian Campus House (CCH) at Northwest Missouri State. In March 2012, they were brainstorming how to reach out to their campus and decided to try offering students rides home, late at night on the weekends. They didn't have a grand vision or end goal in mind—they were just a handful of students, using their own cars to offer safe rides home to their fellow students. At first the ride "schedules" were inconsistent. But when a girl who had received a ride walked up to them in a coffee shop and asked how she could recommend the "Swag Wag" to other students, Garrett knew CCH needed to formalize their idea.

So Garrett got on Twitter and created the @cchswagwag account. Students simply tweet when they need a ride, and the Swag Wag picks them up. Over the past year, their outreach to the campus has exploded. CCH students still use their own cars, offering rides from Thursday to Saturday, from 9 p.m. to 2 a.m., often averaging thirty rides per night.

One of the first groups they helped was a bunch of sorority girls. These girls were extremely appreciative and became friends with the Swag Wag crew, eventually voting to increase their sorority dues so that they could give money to support the Swag Wag. The CCH group thanked the sorority, but the rides were already funded. However, perhaps the sorority would like to support CCH's initiative for clean water in Haiti? The sorority did, and a few of them even joined CCH on their spring break trip to Haiti, where one of the girls came to faith in Christ. Some of the sisters joined a Bible study, and this coming year, there will be a Bible study in their sorority. As one of the sorority sisters said, "I would never have experienced this if you guys hadn't given me a ride home." What a great way to reach a campus. How do you engage the party scene on your campus, if at all?

In the introduction, I told you that college is more than beer and sex, and it's also more than not drinking beer and not having sex. There's so much more to college than participating in or avoiding these two things. Yet on many campuses, the "Animal House" lifestyle is a prominent part of life. Partying, alcohol, sex, and pleasure are pursued with reckless abandon. How can Christians be in that world, but not of it? How can we reach out without being compromised? How can we avoid falling into temptation, especially when it seems like everyone else is doing it? Since alcohol dominates the party and pleasure scene, how should we view it? And since alcohol is so closely connected to sex, what about the culture of hooking up, friends with benefits, and all the other permutations of sexual expression? Let's start by looking at alcohol.

Sedated

A surface treatment of alcohol and college would sound like: "Alcohol is bad; don't drink it." Maybe that's what you heard in health class at school or from your parents or youth ministry. For a young teenager, that's sound advice. But it's not sufficient for the college realm. We have to think about more than behaviors. We need to get under behaviors, because behaviors are simply the surface manifestations of our motives. We need to understand why people indulge in alcohol. What are they looking for?

The slang that people use for getting drunk tells us a lot. People call it getting wasted or they talk about being hammered, wrecked, trashed, smashed, tanked, bombed, obliterated, blitzed, faced, and many other terms I can't print here. Sure, people will usually tell you they're "just having fun." But what kind of fun do these slang terms suggest? It sounds like people are into destruction . . . of themselves. For a night, at least, they are OK with self-destructive behavior. And that's considered fun. Temporarily, it may be. But the worldview underneath it probably isn't.

This is just one place where we see what I call *ideahilism* at work. Ideahilism is a made-up word (as far as I know, I made it up); it combines idealism and nihilism to describe a common college mind-set that by day idealistically wants to save the world, yet by night nihilistically wants to party as if it's ending. Idealists are hopeful that we can make the world a better place, and they work hard to help kids with cancer or dig wells in Africa. Nihilists, on the other hand (particularly moral nihilists), believe that our existence is pointless, and therefore, traditional morality and ethics are arbitrary. Might as well "eat and drink, for tomorrow we die" (1 Corinthians 15:32). Put those two together, and you get *ideahilism*, which doesn't logically make sense at all, but pragmatically feels right to lots of people. Somehow, after a hard day's work in the classroom or for charity, some hedonistic, alcohol-fueled self-destruction seems like a good idea to a lot of people.

We should note that much of the alcohol consumption on our campuses doesn't happen alone. The vast majority of it happens socially. It's encouraged and supported socially. So, again paradoxically, people seek destruction, but in community. It's no wonder that so many students who don't drink, Christian and otherwise, feel excluded from the mainstream of social life on campus. It's no wonder that so many students report that even though they don't like drinking, or it's lost its charm, they continue drinking "because that's what all my friends do" (as multiple students have told me).

So students are seeking self-destructive "fun" in community. What do they actually get out of it? Alcohol abuse isn't new; it's only as old as the first fermented grain or fruit, in all likelihood. The first biblical case of drunkenness is all the way back in Genesis 9 with Noah, but likely predates that. It's an ancient vice.

Let's ask ourselves some wise questions about our relationship with alcohol. These questions are designed to help us bring this area of our lives under the rule of King Jesus, since we're so easily influenced by our friends and the environment. These same questions can be used with regards to drugs.

1. What Has Control? What Has Influence?

Simply being of age doesn't make alcohol indulgence OK. We need to ask about control and influence. Paul speaks to this:

> Be very careful, then, how you live—not as unwise but as wise, making the most of every opportunity, because the days are evil. Therefore do not be foolish, but understand what the Lord's will is. Do not get drunk on wine, which leads to debauchery. Instead, be filled with the Spirit, speaking to one another with psalms, hymns, and songs from the Spirit. Sing and make music from your heart to the Lord, always giving thanks to God the Father for everything, in the name of our Lord Jesus Christ. (Ephesians 5:15-20)

Everyone knows what a DUI is. We're very familiar with the influence of alcohol, and how destructive it can be. Paul's saying the same thing. He's asking, "Who or what are you under the influence of in your life? Alcohol? Adderall?

Something else? Or the Spirit of God?" Christians are to be people under the influence of the Holy Spirit, and nothing else.

2. What's My Motive?

I remember talking with a group of Christian students eager to reach out to the party scene. They were a little too eager, in fact. Their questions had more to do with "How many beers are too many?" and "Is this outfit too inappropriate?" than "How can I love and serve these people and share Jesus with them?" They were more interested in getting their red cup than in sharing Christ. We should always check our motives in areas of temptation. "How far is too far?" is the wrong question, because it asks what we can get away with. Instead of trying to get away with things, let's ask, "How can I glorify God in this situation?" That's your answer, anyway. You know it's too far when you can't glorify God, when you're saying and doing things that reflect badly on him, when you're under other influences, and when your actions don't come from faith. Be ruthless about your motives, because the party scene is alluring. Someone needs to reach out to people in that scene, but it may not be you, or it may not be the time or place for you to reach out.

3. Is It Good for Me?

Just because you can do something doesn't mean you should. Paul had an interesting conversation with the Corinthian church. They were familiar with having a good time, and reasoned, "If I'm permitted to do it, it must be OK." This is another version of "if it feels good, or feels right to you, do it." Paul responded, "'I have the right to do anything,' you say—but not everything is beneficial. 'I have the right to do anything'—but I will not be mastered by anything . . . 'I have the right to do anything'—but not everything is constructive" (1 Corinthians 6:12; 10:23). Goodness trumps rights. Wisdom knows the difference.

4. Does It Help Me Love Others?

Love is the ultimate goal. Even if it's legal for us, there's still the question of how our actions impact others. Is it loving to drink in the face of someone who has a history of abusing it? Or someone who is strongly tempted by it? Paul says about food what we could also say about drink: "Do not destroy the work of God for the sake of food. All food is clean, but it is wrong for a person to eat anything that causes someone else to stumble" (Romans 14:20).

5. How Can I Enter This Redemptively?

A couple of years ago, some students at Shippensburg University in Pennsylvania were frustrated over how to minister within the party scene on their campus. Christians throw around the phrase "in the world but not of it" a lot, and it's a good one (based on the New Testament teaching on how we should approach the world, in John 17:15 and other places). But sometimes it's hard to see how we can be in the party scene world without being of it. So these students, part of a CCO ministry on that campus, resorted to an old staple of college ministry: food. They decided to give away hot dogs—lots of hot dogs. They would set up a grill right off campus and give away hundreds of hot dogs to students going to and from parties. Their ministry soon expanded to include a van service, since safe options for getting home were hard to find. They quickly became known for these giveaways, and their generosity generated many conversations. This ministry has expanded their ability to reach out to the campus.

It's expanded to other campuses, including mine, where we give out what have become known as "Jesus Hot Dogs" on "Christian Corner" (what the recipients have named it), usually about 750 in only two hours on a Friday night. The most common questions are "What's the catch?" and "Why do you guys do this?" both of which allow us to talk about the gospel. We're just trying to figure out how to have a faithful, redemptive presence in the party scenes on our campuses. Jesus is being shared, and we're having a lot of fun doing it.

Hooking Up

Hooking up seems to be a deliberately vague term, ranging from casual making out to full-on sexual intercourse. Alcohol and hooking up often go together. In the book *Hooking Up*, author Kathleen Bogle argues that drinking and hooking up are so closely linked that "students who choose to forgo the party and bar scene are also excluding themselves from the hookup scene."[1] So in this alcohol-infused hookup scene, what are people looking for? I chose to talk about sex here, rather than in the relationships chapter, because the majority of people have disassociated sex and relationship from each other. Sex happens without relationship and vice versa.

But that doesn't mean people aren't looking for connection. I recently read an article about several students at the University of Pennsylvania.[2] One had hoped to find a boyfriend in a more traditional relationship, but quickly realized that the campus environment wasn't conducive to that.

"It's kind of like a spiral," she said. "The girls adapt a little bit, because they stop expecting that they're going to get a boyfriend—because if that's all you're trying to do, you're going to be miserable. But at the same time, they want to, like, have contact with guys." So they hook up and "try not to get attached."

Now, she said, she and her best friend had changed their romantic goals, from finding boyfriends to finding "hookup buddies," which she described as "a guy that we don't actually really like his personality, but we think is really attractive and hot and good in bed."[3]

In other words, they settle for what's available, which is hooking up with people they don't like. Another student, A.,

> enjoyed casual sex on her terms—often late at night, after a few drinks, and never at her place, she noted, because then she would have to wash the sheets . . . from A.'s perspective, she was in charge of her own sexuality.

> "I definitely wouldn't say I've regretted any of my one-night stands," she said.

> "I'm a true feminist," she added. "I'm a strong woman. I know what I want."

> At the same time, she didn't want the number of people she had slept with printed, and she said it was important to her to keep her sexual life separate from her image as a leader at Penn.

> "Ten years from now, no one will remember—I will not remember—who I have slept with," A. said. "But I will remember, like, my transcript, because it's still there. I will remember what I did. I will remember my accomplishments and places my name is hung on campus."[4]

I find this way of thinking to be incredibly sad and tragic. A. is deeply conflicted about her sexuality—on one hand boldly asserting that she knows what she wants, but at the same time trying to keep shame at bay by keeping her sex life separate and secret. I don't believe her when she says she won't remember who she has slept with, and that all she will remember are her accomplishments. That is tragically naive. Life just doesn't work like that. People don't work like that.

The book *Getting Wasted* gives several reasons why alcohol is a part of so many sexual liaisons.[5] Students say it helps them loosen up and overcome inhibitions. It disables their consciences and their judgment. It gives them a built-in excuse for doing dumb things later on because they were "just drunk." And it helps them forget what they've done. As confident as A. seems about her sexual choices, all this "letting go" isn't without its risks. Many colleges are reporting an increase in sexual assault and even rape, very often alcohol-related. Women, for all their newfound confidence in the sexual realm, are still highly vulnerable in these risky, and often demeaning, environments.

One thing we should note is that the problem isn't as simple as students caring about beer and sex too much. It's in this sphere that we also see the impact of other desires becoming too great. Making other things too important, such as grades, career goals, and financial success, may result in the desire for a party "fix." Students believe they must achieve excellent grades to get the job they want, and that they must travel the globe and hop from city to city as part of their personal and professional development. All of which means that they have no ability, time, or interest in settling down with anyone until their late twenties, at the earliest. Meanwhile, they're sexual beings, but they have limited time and energy to meet others, so they settle for booze-infused hookups.

What does it say about the quality of these "relationships" that students don't even *aspire* to have a steady relationship that has the potential to be long-lasting? What does it say that so many people settle for hooking up, and only when they're drunk, with people they don't even like when they're sober? What does it say about how people view themselves and sex when they need to be intoxicated to do it? What does it say when people have reduced another person to a time expenditure, and talk openly of doing a "cost-benefit analysis" over whether or not another person is "worth it"? While the hookup culture allows them some brief companionship and fleeting physical pleasure, it is far, far inferior to what God intended. Let's look at some better options.

Holy Counterculture

There is no other sphere of college life where it is more important for Christians to live as a holy counterculture than in the sex, alcohol, and party scene. We must work together to bring to life a rich and robust alternative. We must show that we are citizens of another kingdom, a better kingdom.

One way that we can assess how to faithfully engage any area is by asking a simple question: Is this something I should reject, receive, or redeem?[6]

Reject: We reject things that are inherently sinful; things that are not something we should or can do in a way that is faithful to Christ. There is no such thing as "Christian stripping," "Christian drug dealing," or "Christian sex trafficking." Those things are to be rejected.

Receive: We receive things that are good and reflect God's common grace to all humankind. We don't eat "Christian food," we eat food, because God causes the sun to rise on the righteous and the unrighteous.

Redeem: We redeem things that God has created good but that have become twisted and perverted in the hands of sinful users. We see this easily in the area of sex. Christians are called to demonstrate how to enjoy this gift in holy, healthy, God-glorifying ways. So let's look at some of what we should reject, receive, and redeem on campus.

Reject: I've made clear above some of the behaviors we're rejecting. We do this because we reject sexual objectification and exploitation as a violation of the dignity and worth that God has put into every person, created in his image. We also reject the worldview of ideahilism, and the debaucherous lifestyle it leads to, because we believe life has a God-given purpose. We reject the overemphasis on pleasure and success that leads to a hookup culture, because there is no amount of success that can justify reducing meaningful relationships to "I'll have time for it when my work is done and I'm drunk." We are relational beings, made by God to have genuine, life-giving relationships with each other, and sex in the context of marriage.

Receive: We can affirm the growing recognition on our campuses that alcohol abuse is a serious issue; that sexual assault is a serious issue; and that risk-taking behavior in both of these areas is a serious issue. Hopefully you and other Christians are encouraging people on your campus who are taking a stand on these things, and coming alongside them in their efforts.

Redeem: When it comes to partying and pleasure, people are seeking good things but in the wrong places and to the wrong degree. What can we offer that's better? What would it look like for Christians to have significant roles in creating the redeemed versions of what they're seeking? For example, people are lonely and looking for friendship and places to connect. Christians should be creating the best, most lasting, most life-giving community on campus. Sadly, many of our groups feel quite cliquish and closed. We settle for superficial relationships much like any other group on campus. Do the lonely find a home among your group and your friends? Are you open and welcoming to the new, the loners, and the strangers? I don't mean simply greeting them and going back to your group; I mean showing hospitality to them and inviting them along in whatever you're doing.

Research on why students drink indicates that they are seeking to escape constant self-awareness. People are highly self-conscious, which is quite burdensome. What if we helped people do that without alcohol, by creating atmospheres where people weren't constantly comparing themselves or sizing each other up? What if we created places where people could forget about themselves and whether or not people accepted them, because they knew they were accepted. This has to go beyond our formal gatherings to the many informal opportunities to hang out during the week—a meal here, a movie there, a game on Saturday afternoon.

Finally, people want to have fun. That is not a bad thing, but often a misguided one. It's my conviction that Christians need to repent of throwing lame parties. Perhaps the most redemptive thing you can do on your campus is throw a better party. This is one way in which we can be "in the world, but not of it." Do it up, and do it big. Make it buzzworthy. For example, on my campus there's a giant fake holiday called State Patty's Day. Students use it as another occasion to drink green beer all day, in addition to the real St. Patrick's Day. It's completely ridiculous. The university and local community have worked hard to curb the partying, but it continues. A few years ago, some of my students came up with an alternative State Patty's Day tour, organizing a series of house parties throughout the day and into the night. Fun locations, interesting people, live music with good bands and good food. We had our own T-shirts and everything, like we were on a bar tour or something. We had fun, and a lot of people came. We had people hanging out with us who had no idea we were Christians, and they had a good time while not hurting themselves or others. These house parties were little lighthouses of grace and truth on what is usually a dark day.

In all these activities, let's remember the point: we are kingdom people, incarnating (living out) the presence of our King. We are seeking to find our ultimate identity, joy, and hope in Jesus Christ. It will be apparent that we have a joy, freedom, and peace that others do not have. Let us make this our prayer:

There are many who say, "Who will show us some good?
Lift up the light of your face upon us, O LORD!"
You have put more joy in my heart
than they have when their grain and wine abound. (Psalm 4:6-7, ESV)

CHAPTER 13

SCRIPTURE STUDY: Discuss the various passages on alcohol use in this chapter.

Discussion Questions

1. Consider the author's term *ideahilism:* "By day, people want to idealistically save the world, yet by night they nihilistically want to party as if it's ending." What are your experiences with ideahilism?

2. When people discuss drinking, they talk about being "hammered, wrecked, trashed, smashed, tanked . . ." What does this language suggest? What makes people so eager to escape reality?

3. This chapter gave some ideas for being "in but not of" your campus social scene: the "Swag Wag," "Jesus hot dogs," etc. What are some creative ways you could reach your campus?

4. What did you think of A.'s story? Do you know students like her? If you could say anything to A., what would it be?

5. What can you reject/receive/redeem on your campus?

Further Reading: *Real Sex,* Lauren Winner

CONCLUSION: KINGDOM COME

My hope and prayer for this book is that it has enlarged your vision for the kingdom of God, and the part God calls you to play in it. I remain convinced that people are looking for hope, community, and purpose, and that through our King and his kingdom, we are given all that we need. You and I need this King, and so does our campus, and so does the world. I hope that I have given you some practical ideas on how to live out your kingdom identity on campus and beyond.

A little while back, the phrase YOLO (You Only Live Once) was all the rage. (I'm sure by the time you read this, YOLO will have gone the way of BMOC.) People tended to use YOLO humorously, like after they do something stupid, writing, "Oh well. #YOLO." This didn't lessen my distaste for the phrase though, because it's not true. Christians know this. We don't only live once; we live forever. And since we live forever—all of us, no matter where we are headed—how should we live? Eternity starts now. The kingdom of God is right here, with you and me, in our midst. As the Psalmist said,

Your kingdom is an everlasting kingdom,
and your dominion endures through all generations.
The Lord is trustworthy in all he promises
and faithful in all he does. (Psalm 145:13)

What we've been discussing doesn't end the day you graduate. Faithful engagement in the mission of God is a lifelong, life-wide calling. So my final question for you is simply this: what's next? How are you going to live out your faith—on campus and beyond? How are you going to be faithful in all these spheres, bringing everything under the rule of King Jesus? While this is the end of the book, it is hopefully just the beginning of lifelong, life-wide faithfulness.

I would love to hear stories about what God is doing in you and through you as you participate in the work of his kingdom. I would love to hear what God is doing on your campus as a result. Feel free to tweet me @stephenlutz, or simply hashtag #KOTC with your thoughts on what you've read here and how you're applying it.

Let's be people who don't withhold a single area of our lives from the King. He is worthy and all things belong to him.

Let's be people who redemptively engage the broken places and people and systems and structures on our campuses, restoring them to God's beautiful, original design.

Let's live as a holy counterculture on our campuses, refusing to bow down to the idols everyone else worships, so that we stand out in our love for the true King.

Let's be people known for both our holiness and wholeness, as we live transformed lives.

Let's be people known for our prevailing prayers and our provocative faith.

Let's be people known for our love for God, each other, and our neighbors.

Let's be people who take every square inch of life seriously, worshiping God in and through all things.

Let's be known for doing things with excellence but not obsessively, keeping things in their proper place before God.

Let's be people known for our good deeds toward others, regardless of how we are treated.

Let's be agents, ambassadors, and citizens of another kingdom, so that our campuses will see an increase in the presence and power of King Jesus.

Let's be people who pray—and live—"Your kingdom come, your will be done, on earth as it is in heaven."

Therefore, since we are receiving a kingdom that cannot be shaken, let us be thankful, and so worship God acceptably with reverence and awe. (Hebrews 12:28)

ENDNOTES

Chapter 1

1. Bruce K. Waltke and Cathi J. Fredricks, *Genesis: A Commentary* (Grand Rapids: Zondervan, 2001), 182.

2. Akkadian, for all you dead language enthusiasts.

Chapter 2

1. C. S. Lewis, "Equality," in *Present Concerns* (Boston, MA: Houghton Mifflin Harcourt), 17.

2. Marianne Bonz, "Religion in the Roman World," Frontline (April 1998), http://www.pbs.org /wgbh/pages/frontline/shows/religion/portrait/religions.html.

Chapter 3

1. Dallas Willard, *The Divine Conspiracy* (New York: HarperCollins, 1997), 403.

2. Rosaria Champagne Butterfield, *Secret Thoughts of an Unlikely Convert: An English Professor's Journey into Christian Faith* (Pittsburgh, PA: Crown & Covenant Publications, 2012).

3. Elvina M. Hall, "Jesus Paid It All" (1865).

4. C. S. Lewis, *Mere Christianity* (New York: Touchstone Books, 1996), 191.

Chapter 4

1. Matt Chandler, *The Explicit Gospel* (Wheaton, IL: Crossway, 2012).

2. C. S. Lewis, *The Weight of Glory: And Other Addresses* (New York: HarperCollins, 2001).

3. With apologies to James L. Hunter and his excellent book, *To Change the World*, I don't think "faithful presence" is the best way to describe how Christians should live in this world. Mere presence sounds far too passive. I prefer "faithful engagement," which captures the sending nature of our mission and the character of Jesus.

Chapter 5

1. R. C. Sproul, *The Holiness of God* (Carol Stream, IL: Tyndale House Publishers, 1998), 42.

2. Dorothy L. Sayers, "The Other Six Deadly Sins," chap. 7 in *Creed or Chaos?* (New York: Harcourt, Brace and Company, 1949).

3. J. C. Ryle, *Wheat or Chaff?* (New York: Robert Carter & Brothers, 1853), 50-51.

4. A. W. Tozer, *The Pursuit of God* (Rockville, MD: Serenity Publishers, 2009), 84.

5. J. C. Ryle, *Holiness: Its Nature, Hindrances, Difficulties, and Roots* (Peabody, MA: Hendrickson Publishers, 2007), 44.

6. Kevin DeYoung, *The Hole in Our Holiness: Filling the Gap between Gospel Passion and the Pursuit of Godliness* (Wheaton, IL: Crossway, 2012), 45.

7. Ibid., 37.

Chapter 6

1. I'm indebted to a Jonathan Edwards sermon, "The Most High—A Prayer-Hearing God," for this summary.

2. I'm indebted to John Smed, a pastor in Vancouver, B.C., and his work on the Lord's Prayer, for much of the material presented here.

3. John Piper, *Let the Nations Be Glad!: The Supremacy of God in Missions* (Grand Rapids: Baker Academic, 2010), 65.

4. Brennan Manning, *The Importance of Being Foolish: How to Think Like Jesus* (New York: HarperCollins, 2005), 128.

Chapter 7

1. It's possible that Bareilles wasn't talking about pushy Christians and evangelistic techniques. Some people think she was talking about her record label. Regardless, the sentiment captures what a lot of people think about evangelism.

2. Jon D. Wilke, "Churchgoers Believe in Sharing Faith, Most Never Do," The Transformational Discipleship Assessment (website), posted August 13, 2012, accessed May 29, 2013, http://tda.lifeway .com/marketing/page/59.

3. A listing of apologetics books and resources I've found helpful in equipping students would be too long to list here. But among the most helpful are Tim Keller's *The Reason for God* and Lee Strobel's *The Case for Faith* and *The Case for Christ*.

4. Is there ever a time for harshness, even anger, in the proclamation of God's truth? The prophets, some of Jesus' teachings, and some of Paul's writings would certainly indicate that. But as a rule of thumb, God saves his harshest words for those who *claim* to be followers of his but are not. He rebukes the hypocrites, the liars, and the religiously self-righteous. His tone toward pagans is remarkably gentle and gracious.

Chapter 8

1. Maltbie Davenport Babcock, "This Is My Father's World" (1901). As found on http://www .hymntime.com/tch/htm/t/i/s/tismyfw.htm.

2. James D. Bratt, *Abraham Kuyper: Modern Calvinist, Christian Democrat* (Grand Rapids: Eerdmans, 2013), 195.

3. Mark A. Noll, Foreword in ibid., ix.

4. Maltbie Davenport Babcock, "This Is My Father's World" (1901). As found on http://www .hymntime.com/tch/htm/t/i/s/tismyfw.htm.

5. Ibid.

Chapter 9

1. Brad House, *Community: Taking Your Small Group Off Life Support* (Wheaton, IL: Crossway, 2011), 89.

2. Dietrich Bonhoeffer, *Life Together* (New York: HarperOne, 1954), 21.

Chapter 10

1. Go Ask Alice! (website), http://goaskalice.columbia.edu

Chapter 11

1. Arum and Roksa, *Academically Adrift* (Chicago: University of Chicago Press, 2010), 91.

Chapter 12

1. Jim Collins, *Good to Great* (New York: HarperCollins, 2001).

2. G. K. Chesterton, *Orthodoxy*. (New York: Dodd, Mead & Co., 1908).

Chapter 13

1. Kathleen A. Bogle, *Hooking Up: Sex, Dating, and Relationships on Campus* (New York: NYU Press, 2008), 167.

2. Kate Taylor, "She Can Play That Game, Too" *New York Times*, published electronically July 12, 2013, http://www.nytimes.com/2013/07/14/fashion/sex-on-campus-she-can-play-that-game-too.html.

3. Ibid.

4. Ibid.

5. Thomas Vander Ven, *Getting Wasted: Why College Students Drink Too Much and Party So Hard* (New York: NYU Press, 2011).

6. This little formula has been encouraged by many pastors and theologians, including, for example, Mark Driscoll.